The **Young Citizen's** [...]
been produced by th[...]
Foundation, an in[...]
educational charity, v[...]
empower individuals[...]
the wider community[...]
education about the law,
democracy and society.

GW00726153

The Citizenship Foundation,
63 Gee Street,
London EC1V 3RS

Tel 020 7566 4141
Fax 020 7566 4131

Email
info@citizenshipfoundation.org.uk

Charity Reg. No. 801360

INDIVIDUALS
ENGAGING IN
SOCIETY

Citizenship Foundation

The Citizenship Foundation would like to thank the **Law Society Charity** for their continued support for this and other projects.

We would also like to thank **The Children's Law Centre**, Belfast, working in the area of children's rights and the law.

We would also like to thank **The Criminal Justice System Northern Ireland** for their support for this project.

Editor and main author Tony Thorpe
Author of the Northern Ireland edition Michael Arlow

Concept devised by Andrew Phillips, Lord Phillips of Sudbury OBE, President of the Citizenship Foundation.

We would like to thank Dan Mace from the Citizenship Foundation and Sarah Witchell, Office of the First Minister and Deputy First Minister, The Department for Agriculture and Rural Development, The Department of Culture, Arts & Leisure, The Department for Employment and Learning, The Department of Education, The Department of Finance and Personnel, The Department of Health, Social Services and Public Safety for their help in adapting this reprinted edition to reflect the law in Northern Ireland.

Also lawyers at Allen & Overy, Linklaters, Lovells, and White & Case for their help in updating the law in this edition.

Designed and illustrated by Nomad Graphique; Mike Gibas, Lena Whitaker, Laura Emms, Mark Askam and Adam Williams.

Photographs AbleStock, Corbis: ©Sean Sexton Collection/Corbis pg 113; ©Geray Sweeney/Corbis pg 115; ©The Scotsman/Corbis Sygma pg 120, PhotoDisc, PhotoAlto, Nomad Graphique, Ingram Publishing

Printed in Dubai

A catalogue record for this title is available from the British Library.

ISBN-10: 0 340 929316
ISBN-13: 978 0340 929315

life

young citizen's **passport**

INDIVIDUALS ENGAGING IN SOCIETY

Citizenship Foundation

sex

Not the whole story

Although sex is discussed much more now than it was in the past, most people at some stage in their lives get confused about what they should and should not be doing. Probably the best advice is:

- **don't believe everything you hear,**
- **decide what feels right for you,**
- **talk to your partner and think about their point of view.**

You don't have to do anything that you are not comfortable with. Nor should you expect your partner to. There is no golden age by which you should have had sex. Some people will choose not to because they are not interested, or because there hasn't yet been the right opportunity, or because they want to wait until they are married. There's plenty of time and it's OK to opt out. Pressurising someone into going further than they want, as well as being morally wrong, can reach a stage where it is also against the law. For example, even kissing or touching someone without their agreement can be an assault. In law, both people must agree to what they are doing (known as consent), and they must understand what is happening. The person who gets someone drunk in order to go to bed with them, or takes advantage of their drunken state, risks being charged with rape. (See **safety**, page 21).

Sex and girls

Age of consent

A girl must be 17 before she can legally have sex with a boy. If she has sex before this, her male partner is breaking the law. Girls cannot be prosecuted for having sex under the age of 17.

The law doesn't usually get involved in punishing girls or women for having sex, although a woman over 17 who has sex with a boy who is under 14' can be prosecuted for indecent assault, even if he consents.

Sex and boys

Unlawful sex

It is an offence for a boy or a man to have sex with a girl under 17 - even if she agrees.

If the girl is under 14, the maximum penalty is life imprisonment, since a girl of 13 or under is assumed by the law not to understand the consequences of having sex. A man who has sex with a girl aged 14-16 can be given a prison sentence of up to two years.

A boy aged 14 or over can be prosecuted for having sex with a girl who is under 13, and it's no defence for the boy to say in court that the girl agreed.

use the law with care **try talking first**

Lesbian and gay relationships

For women

Lesbian relationships are lawful. The law says nothing about lesbianism in general.

For men Gay relationships are lawful if both men consent, are 17 or over and act in private.

For all There are still difficulties for lesbian and gay people in a society where some people and faiths don't fully recognise a person's right to a gay relationship.

Recent changes in the law protect people from discrimination at work on the basis of their sexuality (See **work and training** page 41).

If you need to talk to someone who understands, see **contacts** for groups who may be able to help.

Contraception

Each person who has sex is responsible for guarding against the risks to both people. It is important to know how to use contraceptives properly and how they affect your body. Good advice is therefore vital. For this you can go to a family planning clinic, your doctor or the Brook Advisory Centre, Belfast.

If you're under 16, a doctor can prescribe contraceptives for you without telling your parents - as long as the doctor believes that you are mature enough to understand what is being proposed. Condoms can easily be bought from supermarkets, garages, chemists, from slot machines in toilets and by mail order. Femidoms, which are a form of sheath for women, are sold in chemists. Both these and condoms are available free from family planning clinics.

Emergency contraception is also available to women who are 16 or over to prevent pregnancy up to 72 hours after unprotected sex or contraceptive failure. This is available from some chemists without prescription.

You think you're pregnant

Your period is late and you think you might be pregnant. What do you do? To find out if you are expecting a baby, you can ....

- **see your doctor;**
- **buy a pregnancy testing kit from a chemist. These are generally accurate and cost between £6–£10;**
- **visit a family planning clinic or a Brook Advisory Centre, who will offer confidential advice and provide a free test with an immediate result.**

Help and advice

You are entitled to a confidential consultation with your doctor, no matter what age you are, as long as you say that you do not want your parents to be told. If you are a woman under 16, and you want to have a confidential consultation, at the start of the meeting you should ask your doctor if he or she is prepared to respect your request for confidentiality.

If the doctor is unwilling, help is also available from other organisations such as the fpa, Brook Advisory Centre, or your local family planning clinic.

It is important to do as much as you can to make the right decision. If you can, try to talk also to your partner in pregnancy, your parents and good friends.

Adoption

Giving up a baby for adoption is not easy - for the mother or father. It's best to talk to someone about this, such as your doctor or someone at the antenatal clinic, as soon as possible.

The adoption will probably be handled by a social worker who will discuss the kind of family the birth parents want their child to grow up in and will try to find out as much as possible about the birth family to pass on to the adopters. Adopters usually have to be married.

When the child has settled down with the new family, the adoptive parents can apply for an adoption order, which will be granted if the court is satisfied that all is well.

Neither birth parent has the right to see their child after she or he has been adopted, although the court can give permission for contact and the child can get in touch with them after they are 18. Help and advice for anyone thinking of having their child adopted is available through the local Health and Social Services Trust, Family Care or the Church of Ireland Board for Social Responsibility, see **contacts**.

use the law with care try talking first

ABORTION

In Northern Ireland the circumstances in which an abortion may be carried out are more restricted than those in England, Wales and Scotland. In Northern Ireland abortion is legal only where it is necessary to save the life of the mother or where the continuance of the pregnancy is likely to have serious and long term effects on her mental or physical health.

The decision on whether to have an abortion can have serious moral and long-term consequences. If a person is considering an abortion it is always helpful to talk to someone to find out other options available. This can be a doctor, staff at your local family planning clinic or one of the other organisations listed in the contacts.

Abortion in England, Wales and Scotland follows the law set out in the *Abortion Act 1967*.

This states that an abortion may be legally carried out if two doctors agree that:

- continuing the pregnancy would risk the life of the mother; or
- the mother is less than 24 weeks pregnant and continuation would adversely affect her physical or mental health in a serious or long-term way.

What is HIV?

To understand HIV - standing for human immunodeficiency virus - you have to know something about the immune system that stops us from getting ill.

Blood plays an important part in our body's defence against illness. It contains millions of cells, about one per cent of which are white. A particularly important type of white cell is called the t-helper cell, and one of the jobs of these cells is to fight off infection.

HIV is a virus that attacks the t-helper cells. If it grows inside these cells, and other germs get into our body, we have no way of fighting infection. We become ill and develop what is called acquired immune deficiency syndrome, known as AIDS.

At the moment it is not clear whether everyone who is infected by HIV goes on to develop AIDS.

How do you get HIV?

Let's start with **how you don't get it.** As the virus dies quickly once outside the body, you don't get HIV from

• **hugging • kissing, including French kisses • sharing towels or cutlery • swimming • toilet seats • sharing musical instruments • giving blood.**

The HIV virus is found in the blood, semen, or vaginal fluid of a person with HIV or AIDS. Infection takes place when these fluids pass from an infected person into the bloodstream of someone else. This can happen in several ways:

• **by having unprotected sex with someone who already has the HIV virus. This means putting a penis into a vagina or anus without using a condom. The risk of contracting HIV infection through unprotected oral sex is thought to be much lower - but transmission is possible if semen, vaginal fluid, or menstrual blood come into contact with bleeding gums or mouth infections. You can help to protect yourself from HIV infection through sex by using a condom**

• **by using or sharing a hypodermic needle, which has already been used by someone with HIV, leading to the exchange of a small amount of infected blood**

• **as a result of a mother with HIV passing it on to her baby whilst it is growing inside her.**

Blood transfusions in industrialised countries should be safe as the blood used is routinely screened.

Anyone who feels they may be at risk of HIV or AIDS should seek medical advice and help, see **contacts**.

SEXUALLY TRANSMITTED INFECTIONS (STIs)

Sexually transmitted infections (also called venereal disease, VD or the clap) are caught from sexual contact with people who have the infection themselves. Most STIs can be cured if treated as soon as possible, and so if you have had sex and you have sores or pain around your sexual organs, see a doctor straightaway. Don't have sex with anyone until it's cleared up, because you will put your partner's health at risk too.

However, not all STIs show signs of infection. Anyone who has sex with someone who is not their regular partner is at risk, particularly if they fail to use a condom. Chlamydia, for example, can pass undetected for some time, but may eventually produce pain and discomfort, and cause infertility in men and give women problems in conceiving.

Advice and treatment on sexually transmitted infections is available from clinics dealing with family planning, pregnancy or genito-urinary medicine, as well as family doctors. It is entirely confidential, although if you are under 16, the doctor may be reluctant to do anything without consulting your parents. If this is the case, it is worth checking first.

HIV and work

If you have HIV or AIDS, you are under no obligation to tell your employer. However, the government advises any health care worker who believes themselves to be at risk from infection to seek medical advice immediately. Your employer has a legal duty to treat the information that you are HIV positive as confidential. As a rule, employers are not entitled to tell other workers that an employee is infected with HIV, without his or her permission.

Employers may, if they wish, ask all those who apply for a job to take an HIV test. They cannot insist on existing employees taking a test, unless it is already in their contract. But if you apply for a job and the firm discovers that you are HIV positive they are quite within their rights to turn you down. If you lie about it, and they realise you are HIV positive after you have begun work, you may be dismissed.

If you are worried about HIV or AIDS, support and help is available, see **contacts**.

Prostitution

Prostitutes sell sex for money. They can be either men or women. It is an offence for a prostitute to attract "business" in public (called soliciting) and for someone to try to obtain the services of a prostitute from a motor vehicle that they are in, or have just got out of. Under the *Sexual Offences Act 2003*, it is an offence for a person to pay for sex with someone under 18.

If the police become aware that a young person under the age of 18 is involved in prostitution, they will almost certainly inform Social Services who will decide whether to apply for an order to take that person into care.

drugs and the law

Controlled drugs

All drugs produce some kind of change in the way a person's body or mind works, and the availability of most drugs - whether aspirins, alcohol or amphetamines - is controlled by law.

The main law covering the use of dangerous drugs in the United Kingdom is the *Misuse of Drugs Act 1971*. Under this Act, drugs that people might misuse have been placed on a list of controlled drugs, and it is an offence to possess, produce or supply anyone with them. The list of controlled drugs is divided into three categories - Classes A, B and C.

CLASS A DRUGS

Cocaine is a white powder sometimes injected, but usually snorted, through a tube. Crack is cocaine treated with chemicals, so it can be smoked. Both give a high, followed by a rapid down. The only way to maintain the high is to keep taking the drug - but regular use leads to sickness, sleeplessness, weight loss, and addiction.

Heroin is made from the opium poppy - smoked, sniffed or injected. It comes as a white powder when pure. Street heroin is usually brownish white. Heroin slows down the brain and, at first, gives a feeling of total relaxation. Repeated use creates dependency. Overdosing causes unconsciousness and often death - particularly if used with other drugs, such as alcohol.

CLASS B DRUGS

Amphetamines sold as pills or powder, were developed to treat depression. They give a feeling of energy and confidence, but increasing doses are needed to keep up the effect. The downside is anxiety, insomnia, irritability and less resistance to disease and, as with all illegal drugs, there is no guarantee that they do not contain other harmful substances.

Barbiturates are used in medicine to help people who cannot sleep. They produce feelings of drowsiness and relief from anxiety. Sold as a powder or coloured capsule. Regular use creates dependency. Extremely dangerous when taken with alcohol or other drugs.

LSD, also known as acid, is a man-made substance, sold impregnated on blotting paper (often printed with cartoon characters or in colourful patterns) and dissolved on the tongue. It usually takes about an hour to work, and lasts up to 12 hours. The effects depend on the strength of the dose and the user's mood. It generally distorts feelings, vision and hearing, and bad trips lead to depression and panic, or worse, if the user is already anxious.

Ecstasy, or E, is sold as tablets of different shapes and colour. It makes the user feel friendly and full of energy, and sound and colours can seem much more intense. However, the comedown can leave the user tired and low - often for days. Regular users can have problems sleeping, and some women find it makes their periods heavier. Ecstasy affects the body's temperature control and it may cause the user to overheat and dehydrate. There is no guarantee that tablets sold as ecstasy do not contain some other ingredients. This can make their use unpredictable and dangerous.

Magic mushrooms contain hallucinogenic chemicals on the list of controlled drugs. It is not against the law to pick them fresh, but it is against the law to grow or prepare them in any way, or to possess them with the intention of supplying them to someone else. Most commonly used are the Liberty Cap and Fly Agaric. The effects similar to a mild dose of LSD, with high blood pressure and possible stomach pains and vomiting. The greatest danger is in eating highly poisonous mushrooms, mistaking them for the hallucinogenic kind.

CLASS C DRUGS

Tranquillisers cause lower alertness, and affect people who drive or operate machinery. A number of anabolic steroids are also on the list of controlled drugs after concern over their misuse in sport and bodybuilding.

Although cannabis has recently been classified as a Class C drug, possession and supply remain illegal. Anyone over 18 on their first occasion found in possession or using cannabis is liable to arrest and may receive a warning or an official caution and the drug will be confiscated. Smoking cannabis in public or near a place where there will be children will be viewed as 'aggravated circumstances' and arrest is likely. Those found repeatedly committing an offence are likely to face arrest and prosecution. Under 18 year olds found in possession of class C drugs are likely to be referred to the Youth Diversion Office, through whom they are likely to either receive a restorative caution or an informed warning.

Cannabis comes in a solid dark lump, known as resin, or as dried leaves, called grass. The effects vary from one person to another. Some feel relaxed and happy, but the downside can be moodiness, anxiety, and difficulties with memory. Heavy users risk great tiredness, mental heath problems, and cancer - from the chemical constituents.

drugs and the law

The risks

- **There is no way of knowing exactly what is in drugs made or obtained illegally. This makes them unpredictable and dangerous.**
- All drugs have side effects that may be dangerous and even fatal - particularly if they are mixed or taken regularly.
- Anyone using shared needles, filters or spoons, risks becoming infected with hepatitis or HIV, the virus that leads to AIDS.
- Employers and head teachers have a legal duty to confiscate drugs found at work or school and hand them to the police as quickly as possible.
- Illegal drug taking places a person's job, school, or college place at risk.
- A person prosecuted for illegal drug use will not necessarily be sent to prison, but could end up with a criminal record. However, a prison sentence is a strong possibility for someone found guilty of supply.

Possession

Possession of a controlled drug is an offence, even if it's only a tiny amount. First-time offenders in possession of Class C drugs are likely to receive a reprimand or warning. Repeat offenders and users who smoke cannabis in public may be taken to court.

Supply

It is an offence under the *Misuse of Drugs Act 1971* to supply or to offer to supply someone with a controlled drug. Obviously this includes the sale of drugs - but it is still an offence even if money does not change hands. Giving a controlled drug to a friend or sharing a drug at a party by passing it from one person to another is still seen in law as supply. (See **leisure**, page 85)

It is also an offence if the substance sold is not actually a controlled drug, but the seller claimed or believed it to be one.

Production

It is an offence under the *Misuse of Drugs Act 1971* to produce any controlled drug. This includes letting someone use your kitchen or a room for this purpose.

Growing cannabis comes under this heading, and is an offence if you knew what you were doing.

use the law with care try talking first

BRIEF CASE: Dennis

Dennis bought 1,000 tabs of what he thought was LSD, and was caught by the police trying to sell them. When the tablets were analysed they were found not to contain LSD, but a harmless vegetable product that was not at all illegal. Despite this, Dennis was accused and found guilty of supplying an illegal or controlled drug, because his intention was to supply LSD.

Police powers

If a police officer has reasonable grounds to suspect that someone is in possession of a controlled drug, the officer can search that person and their vehicle and seize anything that seems to be evidence of an offence.

Glue sniffing

The effect of solvent abuse is rather like getting drunk on alcohol. However, it takes effect more quickly as the substances enter the bloodstream through the lungs rather than the stomach. Sniffers may experience hallucinations and, if plastic bags are used, may become unconscious or choke on their own vomit. Glue sniffing itself is not against the law, but it is an offence, under the *Intoxicating Substances (Supply) Act 1985* to supply a solvent to a young person under 18 if there is reasonable cause to believe that the fumes might be inhaled.

It is also an offence to sell lighter fuel to anyone under 18.

Tobacco and alcohol

Tobacco should not be sold by law to anyone who seems to be under the age of 16. Under the *Children and Young Persons (Protection from Tobacco) NI Order 1991*, shopkeepers can be fined up to £2,500 for selling tobacco or cigarettes to under-age children. In Northern Ireland, district councils, in cooperation with the police, operate schemes to discourage young people under 16 from smoking in public places. There has been some discussion about raising the age limit for tobacco sales to 18, but there are, as yet, no firm proposals to change the law.

For details of the law and alcohol, see **leisure**, pages 80-81.

Information

Free publications on all drugs and solvents are available from most libraries. The National Drugs Helpline is open 24 hours a day, every day of the year, tel (free) 0800 77 66 00 or email frank@talktofrank.com

BRIEF CASE: Alex

Alex was one of a group who bought and sold drugs for themselves and other students at their university. One day, his friend Paul took an overdose of heroin and died. It was Alex who had supplied the drug. A court sentenced him to five years in prison.

health

Doctors

Confidentiality and consent

Once you're 16, you can decide about your own health care. A person under 16 can agree to their own medical treatment if the doctor believes that they fully understand what is being proposed. Patients also have a right of confidentiality. Doctors should not usually pass on what they say or what treatment they are having unless they agree.

General practitioners Everyone living in the UK, including visitors from overseas, is entitled to register with a GP practice. A list of local doctors is available from your local Health and Social Services Board, Health and Social Services Council, the Central Services Agency, main post office, library, tourist information office, and Citizens Advice Bureau.

You have the right to change your GP at any time. You don't have to explain your reasons for doing so or tell the doctor concerned. However, a doctor does not have to accept you as a patient either. If you are refused in this way, the Health and Social Services Board has a duty to give you details of local GPs within two working days. New patients are entitled to a health examination when they join a practice.

If you are staying for up to three months in another part of the United Kingdom, you can ask to be registered with another GP practice on a temporary basis. But if you are leaving home and going to college or university it's probably better to register with a new doctor in the town or city where you are staying, so you are guaranteed all the services of the practice if you ever need them. It's helpful to provide your medical card or National Health number when you register. If you don't have these, you will need to know your place of birth and the name and address of the doctor or practice with which you were previously registered.

PRESCRIPTIONS

Prescriptions are free if you:
- **are under 16;**
- **are 16, 17 or 18 and in full-time education;**
- **are pregnant or have had a baby in the last 12 months;**
- **suffer from a certain specified serious illness;**
- **or your partner receive Income Support, income-based Jobseeker's Allowance, Pension Credit Guarantee Credit or Tax Credits; or**
- **your name is on a current HC2 certificate.**

Further details are available from GPs, the Citizens Advice Bureau and from libraries.

Anyone now claiming a free prescription will be asked to provide proof that they are entitled to do so. A person who cannot do this should not be refused the prescription, but a check on their entitlement may be made by the Counter Fraud Unit of the Central Services Agency.

use the law with care try talking first

Records Under the *Data Protection Act 1998*, you have a general right to see all your medical records – whether they are held on paper or computer. You are also entitled to ask for a copy to take away. Access however may be refused if the doctor believes that seeing your records may cause you or someone else serious physical or mental harm.

Your GP or the hospital may ask you to pay for this service. The maximum charge to see your records (either on paper or on screen) is £10. The maximum charge for a copy of a computer held record is also £10 – and £50 for records held manually.

If you believe that the information on your records is not correct, you may ask for it to be changed. The doctor, however, does not have to accept your opinion, but is required to note on your records what you have said.

DENTISTS

Health Service dentists now operate a care package for all their Health Service registered patients. This care programme, requires patients to attend for a checkup or treatment at least once every 15 months. Patients who do not keep in touch with their dentist over this period risk losing their entitlement to Health Service care with that dentist. Once a dentist accepts a patient for a continuing care programme, the patient must be provided with all the treatment necessary for dental health, on the Health Service.

Before each course of treatment, you will receive a treatment plan, showing the work the dentist intends to carry out and what it will cost (if you have to pay). The dentist may offer to treat you privately, but should not place pressure on you by implying that the treatment is not available on the Health Service. You do not have to accept the treatment being offered.

If you wish to change your dentist, the local Health and Social Services Board should, within five working days, be able to find you a dentist who can give you Health Service treatment.

If you need emergency treatment, but are not registered for continuing care, you should contact a local Health Service dentist to see if he or she is prepared to accept you on an emergency basis. If they can't, contact your local Health and Social Services Board, who should be able to find a dentist prepared to provide treatment. Some Boards operate relief of pain clinics during evenings, weekends and bank holidays.

Charges are made for most dental treatment. But dental treatment is free if:

- you are under 18 or aged 18 and in full-time education;
- you are pregnant or have had a baby or still born baby in the previous 12 months;
- you or your partner receive Income Support, income-based Jobseeker's Allowance, Tax Credits or Pension Credit Guarantee Credit (PCGC); or
- your name is on a valid HC2 charges certificate.

If you don't qualify for free dental treatment or help with the cost, you must pay up to 80% of the cost, up to a maximum of £384 (May 2006).

Dentists can charge a patient who fails to keep an appointment or cancels at very short notice. The level of charge varies from one dentist to another.

health

Opticians Eye tests are no longer free to everyone. You will get a free test if you:

- **are under 16;**
- **are 16, 17 or 18 and in full-time education;**
- **are registered blind or partially sighted;**
- **or your partner receive Income Support, income-based Jobseeker's Allowance, Tax Credits or PCGC; or**
- **your name is on a valid HC2 Charges certificate**

If you need glasses you may be entitled to help with buying them, particularly if you are unemployed or a student on a low income. Further information is available from opticians, the Citizens Advice Bureau and booklet HC11, *Help with health costs*, available from libraries.

Complaints Health and Social Services Boards and Councils provide leaflets which explain what to do if you have a complaint about the health or social services, and how it should be dealt with. These leaflets are often available from GPs, hospitals, dentists and opticians.

If you have a complaint about your treatment, it's important to make it as

soon as possible. Generally, six months is allowed from the date of the incident or the discovery of the problem, as long as it is within 12 months of the initial event.

Tattoos It's illegal for a person to be given a tattoo if they are under 18.

The right to die The law states that a doctor may give a patient a painkilling drug, which shortens their life, as long as the intention is to relieve pain and suffering and not to kill. If the drug is given with the intention of ending that person's life, the doctor can face a charge of murder.

It is possible to make what is called a living will (known in law as an advance directive) setting out how you would like to be treated if you ever lose the capacity to make or convey a decision. You must clearly understand what you are doing when you give the directive and, if it is done properly, it is legally binding on the doctor. But an advance directive cannot authorise a doctor to do anything unlawful.

Wills Anyone aged 18 or over can make a will, provided they are capable of understanding what they are doing. There is no lower age limit for people in the forces on active service, or sailors at sea.

Blood There's no legal minimum age to become a blood donor, but the Northern Ireland Blood Transfusion Service won't accept anyone under 17. Donors usually give about three quarters of a pint twice a year.

ADVICE

Information on health provision in Northern Ireland may be found at www.n-i.nhs.uk, or through the Central Services Agency, see contacts.
Health and Social Services Boards and Councils have a range of leaflets which provide information on matters related to health and health provision. Here you may find information about the standard of service that you should receive from your local hospital, doctor, dentist, optician, chemist and other community health workers.

safety

young citizen's passport

INDIVIDUALS ENGAGING IN SOCIETY

Citizenship Foundation

violent crime

Fighting Back

If you're threatened or hit, it's usually better to try to avoid a fight by talking to your attacker or backing off calmly.

If you can't do this, the law says that you can use reasonable force to defend yourself. This means that you're entitled to fight back, but not to go over the top and beat up the other person. If you do, you will have also committed an offence.

There is no law that says that you must report a crime to the police. If you want to claim compensation for your injuries the crime must first have been reported to the police.

Arrest – doing it yourself

If you see someone committing a serious offence or have reasonable grounds for believing that they have committed one, you can make a citizen's arrest. But, take care. People have been hurt and even killed trying to do their civic duty. The best advice is to take in as much as you can about the incident, and then to ring the police. If you do get involved, remember that an ordinary person only has the power to make an arrest for a serious offence - such as theft, serious assault, or burglary. Don't arrest someone for parking on a double yellow line.

Neighbourhood patrols also come up against this problem. They can't arrest someone who they think is about to commit an offence (it must already have been done), nor can they use excessive force - otherwise they can face charges of assault and wrongful arrest.

Victims of violent crime

Victims of violent crime can apply to the *Compensation Agency* for compensation for their injuries - which must be serious enough to receive an award. The crime must be reported to the police without delay, and an application for compensation made within two years of the incident that caused the injury. However, all cases are treated individually and an exception can be made if, for example, the delay in reporting was caused by the after effects of the crime.

Victim Support runs a helpline and advice to victims of crime. Their number is in the local phone book. See **contacts**, page 134.

If you are a victim of crime and called as a witness, you can arrange to see a courtroom before the case starts, have a seat reserved for someone accompanying you and ask to wait separately from other people. Details are given in Victims of Crime – a Code of Practice and the Courts' Charter for Northern Ireland. See **contacts**.

■ BRIEF CASE: Raj

Raj ran an off-licence, and had twice been the victim of armed robbery. One night, a man carrying a long knife came into the shop demanding money from the till. As Raj was being held with a knife to his throat, his brother came through from the back and the robber ran off. Raj was so angry that he got into his van and chased the man down the street knocking him down and killing him. Raj was found guilty of manslaughter and sentenced to two and a half years imprisonment. The Court decided that he could not have been acting in self-defence because he was, by that time, not being attacked or threatened.

use the law with care **try talking first**

Self defence If you carry something to use for self-defence, you run the risk of actually breaking the law yourself. Under the *Prevention of Crime Act 1953*, it is an offence to carry something made, or adapted, to cause injury to someone. This includes things like a knife, bicycle chain, or a sharpened comb. The penalty is a prison sentence or a heavy fine.

Knives In general, it is an offence to have a firearm or anything with a blade or sharp point in a public place. Folded pocket knives are allowed as long as the blade is less than 3" long and does not have a lock on it. Schools are specifically mentioned as places where articles with blades or points must not be carried, and the police have the power to enter and search school premises if they have a good reason to believe that an offence of this kind has been committed. The penalty is a prison sentence or a fine.

SOME WORDS THEY USE

Assault & battery The word assault is not used in law in quite the same way as in everyday speech. Strictly speaking, an assault takes place when someone causes a person to fear that they are about to suffer immediate unlawful physical violence. Battery is the act of actually hitting that person or using force (even very little force) on them without their consent. Normally assault and battery take place at the same time. But it is possible to be assaulted without battery (raising an arm and shouting threats without hitting anyone), and to be battered without assault (hitting someone from behind without warning).

Burglary Burglary takes place when a person enters a building without permission, intending to steal, cause unlawful damage, seriously harm or rape someone. Even if nothing is taken or done, a crime has still been committed. It's enough in law to prove that the person intended to break the law in this way.

Robbery Stealing something with the use or threat of force.

Theft There are, in law, three parts to theft. A person is guilty of theft who
(i) dishonestly takes something, which
(ii) belongs to someone else, and
(iii) intends to deprive that person of it permanently.

harassment

Abusive behaviour

Under the *Public (NI) Order 1987*, it is an offence to use abusive or insulting words or behaviour in public in a way that is intended to cause a person harassment, alarm, or distress. It's also an offence to put up a sign or a poster that is threatening or abusive in the same way. The law is designed to protect anyone who is being treated like this because, for example, of their religion, race, disability or sexuality. Harassment of this kind is a crime - just like any other - and can be reported to the police, who have a duty to investigate and to try to find those responsible. Statements from witnesses will strengthen a case.

The NI Housing Executive also has a number of powers it can use to help tenants or homeowners in their area who are being harassed or attacked. They can take action against residents for harassing or causing nuisance to other residents, and can obtain a court order stopping people committing certain types of anti-social behaviour. If those responsible are tenants, the Executive may be able to evict them from their home.

The Housing Executive, the police and the district council can apply for Anti-Social Behaviour Orders.

Stalking

The *Protection from Harassment (NI) Order 1997* became law after a number of cases involving men following women over a considerable period of time. It is now an offence for someone to behave in a way that they know (or ought to know) amounts to harassment or puts a person in fear of violence being used against them. For an offence to be committed, the behaviour or conduct must take place on at least two occasions and is punishable by imprisonment and/or a fine.

Someone who feels they might be a victim of harassment can apply to a court, for what is known as an injunction, ordering the person committing the offence to keep a certain distance from the victim's house or place of work. The victim can also apply for compensation for the worry they have suffered or for loss of earnings through time off work.

■ BRIEF CASE: Marcia

Marcia and her 10-year old son were not the only black people on their estate, but for some reason faced almost continuous trouble from one particular group of boys. Marcia first tried ignoring the problem and then spoke to the boys and tried to talk to their parents. Nothing worked. Eventually she complained to the council who investigated the case and obtained a court order requiring the parents of one of the boys to leave their house, which they rented from the council. The boy's parents appealed, saying it was not their offensive behaviour but that of their son. The appeal was dismissed. The judge said that Marcia and her son should not be deprived of their rights just because the parents could not control their son.

use the law with care try talking first

What if it happens to me? It all depends on the situation. If it's an isolated incident and the person is someone you don't know, then it may be best to try and ignore it. If you react and get abusive yourself, you run the risk of finding yourself in a far worse situation.

However, if it's happened before, or you're being harassed where you live, then it's important to tell the police - for your own safety. If you are getting abuse at school, college or at work, try and sort it out with the people concerned, but if that's not possible, or successful, raise it with someone in authority, who will have a legal duty to help you. See also the section on **discrimination** page 41.

Someone suffering serious abuse or harassment may be able to claim compensation from the Compensation Agency (see page 18) and **contacts**.

sexual assault

Indecent assault Under the *Offences Against the Person Act 1861*, it is an offence to touch or threaten a person in an indecent way. Groping and unwanted fondling can come into this category. Indecent assault carries a punishment of up to ten years' imprisonment.

Rape A male who has either vaginal or anal intercourse with someone who doesn't want him to and who knows or doesn't care that this person is not consenting, commits the crime of rape. It's also an offence to threaten or force a person to have sex against their will, or to give them drugs in the hope that they will give in.

Going out with someone is not, in law, an invitation to have sexual intercourse with them. Forcing another person to have sex is rape, and it's no defence for the man to say that he was drunk.

It's also rape if the victim had too much alcohol or other drugs to know what they were doing. A wife doesn't have to have sex with her husband. If she does not consent, it's rape (see page 114).

If you are raped Although you may not want to tell anyone, most police stations now have women officers who have been trained to deal with victims of sexual offences in a sensitive way. If you are a woman, you can ask to be examined by a female doctor and you can take along your parents or a friend.

sexual assault

The police will be able to gather evidence more easily if you report the rape or assault as soon as possible. Reporting the crime early also makes your evidence more believable in court.

Once a victim tells the police that they have been raped or sexually assaulted, or the suspect has been charged, the victim has the right in law to remain anonymous. The victim cannot be questioned in court by the accused, nor can their name and address or picture be reported in the media. Attempted rape is dealt with in the same way.

Help is available from *Victim Support* and the local *Rape Crisis Centre*, who will talk to any girl or woman who has suffered an unpleasant sexual experience. *Survivors* offer an advice service for men, see **contacts**. Victims of rape can apply for compensation to the *Compensation Agency*, see **contacts**.

Male victims of rape are treated in law in the same way as female victims.

Accused of rape If you are accused of raping someone, immediately contact a solicitor. Rape is a serious crime, and the punishment can be severe.

keeping safe

There are some simple steps that both men and women can take to make themselves safer.

- **If you go out - especially at night - tell someone where you are going. If possible, stay away from known danger spots.**
- **If you're out late, get a lift back if you can with someone you trust, or book a taxi, see page 84.**
- **If you walk home, try to get someone to go with you.**
- **Check on the security of your home. Ordinary bolts and chains are not expensive.**
- **Knowing some self-defence can give you a feeling of greater confidence.**
- **If you carry a screech alarm keep it ready in your hand, not in your pocket or handbag.**
- **Men can help by taking care not to frighten women. For example, if you're walking in the same direction as a woman at night, don't walk behind her, cross over the road and walk on the other side.**
- **If you are facing some kind of harassment, tell someone about it. Ignoring it can make you more vulnerable.**

Abusive telephone calls It is an offence to make malicious and threatening phone calls with a prison sentence and a heavy fine.

If you get such a call, try not to react and don't start talking to the caller. Don't hang up, but put the receiver down and walk away for a few minutes. Try to do something else, and then put the handset back without checking if the caller is still there. If the phone rings again, pick up the receiver and don't say anything - a genuine caller will speak first. Advice on dealing with calls of this kind is available from BT, tel free 0800 666 700.

education

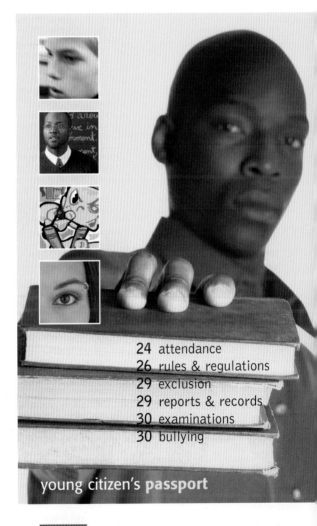

young citizen's **passport**

INDIVIDUALS
ENGAGING IN
SOCIETY

Citizenship Foundation

attendance

Parents have the main responsibility, in law, for their child's education. Under the *Education and Libraries (NI) Order 1986*, it is the duty of parents with children of compulsory school age, to make sure that their child has 'an efficient full-time education suitable to his age, ability and aptitude... by regular attendance at school or otherwise.'

The word 'otherwise' is important here because it allows parents to educate their children out of school. They do not need permission from the Education and Library Board to do this, but do have to satisfy the relevant Board that the education is efficient, full-time and suitable and must de-register their child if they are already in school.

Which school?

Under the *Education and Libraries (NI) Order 1986*, parents can choose the school they would like their child to attend, and the Department of Education and the Education and Library Boards must follow this wish if possible. But parents may be refused their choice if the school is full, or if it is felt that their choice would be an inefficient, or unreasonably expensive way of educating their child.

If admission to a particular school is refused, parents (but not pupils) have a right of appeal against the decision and should be told how to go about this in the letter of refusal.

Parents who cannot agree between themselves on a choice of school can ask a court to decide where their child will be educated. In this situation, the court must take account of the wishes and feelings of the child concerned.

■ BRIEF CASE: Peter

After their divorce, Peter's parents couldn't agree about where he should go to school. His mother wanted him to attend a boarding school, his father (with whom Peter lived) said that he couldn't afford the fees and felt Peter should go to a day school. Peter's mother asked a court to decide on her son's future education.

After hearing from both parents, the judge decided that Peter's father could well afford the school fees and so Peter should go to the boarding school. However his father appealed against this, saying that no one in court had asked Peter what he wanted.

The Court of Appeal did just this. Peter, who was 14, told the Court that he wanted to live with his father and couldn't do so if he was at boarding school. The Court of Appeal felt that it was important to take Peter's wishes into account, and said he could go to the school of his choice.

Costs

State education is free and it is unlawful for schools to try to make parents pay for books or equipment that pupils need for subjects or activities taken in school hours as part of the National Curriculum. However, charges may be made for…

- **individual music tuition;**
- **materials for practical subjects (if the pupil wants to keep the finished product);**
- **optional trips taken outside school hours;**
- **board and lodging on school trips, even if the activity is part of the school timetable.**

use the law with care try talking first

Parents who receive Disability Working Allowance, Family Credit, Income Support or income based Jobseeker's Allowance need not pay any of these charges.

Grammar Schools in Northern Ireland may make some additional charges.

The local Education and Library Board has a duty to provide pupils with free school transport or passes if their school is not within 'walking distance' (two miles in primary school, three miles in post-primary school) from the pupils' homes. This only applies if the parents have been unsuccessful in gaining a place for their child at all the suitable schools within walking distance.

Pupils at school, below the age of 19, are entitled to free school meals if their parents receive Income Support or income-based Jobseeker's Allowance or in certain circumstances, the Child Tax Credit. Pupils who bring a packed lunch, must be provided with somewhere comfortable to eat it.

Leaving school or staying on

Under the *Education and Libraries (NI) Order 1986*, compulsory school age begins in the September following the child's fourth birthday, but a child born in July or August will not start until the September after their fifth birthday. Compulsory schooling ends on the 30th June following the child's sixteenth birthday, but pupils who are 16 between 2nd July and 31st August cannot leave school until the 30th of June the following year.

A parent cannot force their child who has passed compulsory school age to stay on at school against their wishes.

attendance

Truancy

Parents have a legal duty to make sure that their child attends school regularly or is suitably educated elsewhere. If they fail to do this they may be committing a criminal offence – and it is no defence for them to say that they didn't know their child was truanting or that they could do nothing to force them to attend. A parent may be fined if their child does not attend school.

An Education Welfare Officer works with parents to try to ensure their child attends school. The Education and Library Board can get a number of court orders to help with this, these are called Attendance Orders (AOs) and Education Supervision Orders (ESOs). When an ESO is made, an education supervisor will be appointed for the child. It is their duty to advise and help the child, they can also give directions to parents in order to ensure that the child is properly educated.

Ultimately a child who is still not attending school, even after an ESO has been made, can be taken into the care of the local Health and Social Services Trust, which then takes responsibility for ensuring the child receives an education.

Further education

If you decide to stay on at school or go to a college of Further Education from September 2006, you may be able to get an Education Maintenance Allowance (EMA). EMA is a fortnightly payment of up to £60 for students who are aged 16 ,17 or 18 years on or between 2nd July 2005 and 1st July 2006. It is paid directly to young people from households with an income of £30,810 or less who stay on in education after tthe end of their compulsory schooling.

Details are avaible from your school, college or JobCentre/Jobs & Benefits Office. Alternatively you can ring the Customer Service Team on 0845 601 7646.

Higher education

From 2006, universities and colleges in the UK will start charging tuition fees of up to £3,000 a year.

Wherever you decide to study in Northern Ireland or elsewhere in the UK, you will not have to pay these fees before or whilst you are studying. All eligible Northern Ireland students studying full-time can get a loan of up to £3,000 a year to meet their course costs. This loan does not have to be repaid until you have left university and are earning more than £15,000 a year.

The amount of fees charged will vary between courses as well as colleges. It is important to compare what's on offer and which course suits you best. A good source of information is the university's or college's own website or prospectus.

A student loan for maintenance/living costs will help you pay for expenses such as accommodation, food and course materials. This is additional to the student loan available to cover the cost of fees. Details are available from your local Education and Library Board. Also see **www.studentfinanceni.co.uk**

Religious worship and education

The *Education and Libraries (NI) Order 1986* requires all grant-aided schools to have a period of collective worship each day. In state schools this act of worship must not be distinctive of any particular religious denomination.

The law states that all grant-aided schools must provide religious education as part of their curriculum. Parents may request that their child be wholly or partly excused from attendance at religious instruction or collective worship or both. This must not interfere with the attendance of the pupil at school.

Pupils cannot opt out of religious education or worship themselves, it must be done by their parents.

Sex education

The law states that schools must prepare pupils for the 'responsibilities and experiences of adult life'. This should mean that schools provide pupils with education about sex and gender issues. The Department of Education has issued guidance to all schools on sex education. The guidance states that sex education should be an important element in the curriculum and should be taught in a

use the law with care try talking first

sensitive manner, in harmony with the ethos of the school or college, and in conformity with the moral and religious principles held by parents. In practice most schools in Northern Ireland seek parental consent before giving a child sex education. The law in Northern Ireland does not give clear guidance on the rights of children and parents in the area of sex education.

Punishment

Teachers are entitled to impose punishments - but these must be reasonable.

The *Education (NI) Order 1998* allows a school to keep a pupil under 18 in detention after school even though the pupil's parents may not agree. However, the detention must be reasonable in the circumstances and the pupil's parents must have been given at least 24 hours notice of the detention in writing.

Pupils should not be held in detention for too long, nor should their safety be put at risk, e.g. if, as a consequence, they miss the last bus home.

Discipline

Schools must, by law, have their discipline policy available in writing, and must make sure it is brought to the attention of all parents.

School uniform

Schools are entitled to insist that pupils wear a particular uniform, as long as it is reasonable and does not discriminate on grounds of sex or race. Pupils can be excluded from school if they persistently break the rules over uniform unless this is because of genuine religious or cultural reasons. Parents of pupils who are repeatedly sent home for not wearing the correct uniform may be prosecuted for failing to ensure their child regularly attends school.

Confiscation

Teachers may confiscate any forbidden items, such as mobile phones, jewellery etc., which they should keep safe and return to the pupil after a reasonable time.

If illegal drugs or weapons are found, teachers must confiscate the items and may hand them over to the police.

CORPORAL PUNISHMENT

Corporal punishment is now banned in all schools in Northern Ireland. Under the *Education (NI) Order 1998* a member of staff in a school can use reasonable force to prevent a pupil from:

- **committing an offence;**
- **injuring someone or damaging property; or**
- **behaving in a way that threatens the good order and discipline at the school.**

However, if a teacher goes beyond what is reasonable, he or she may have committed an assault, which can give rise to both criminal charges and a civil claim for damages.

DRUGS IN SCHOOL

Schools are required to make clear to pupils and parents what action will be taken if pupils are found to be involved in any way with unauthorised drugs within the boundaries of the school. The term "unauthorised drugs" includes tobacco, alcohol, as well as illegal drugs, such as cannabis and cocaine, and the "boundaries of the school" may include journeys to and from school, work experience, and school trips.

The law The law allows school staff to take temporary possession of a substance suspected of being an illegal drug, but they are not allowed to carry out personal searches. Staff should persuade pupils to hand over any drugs voluntarily, and if a personal search is required, the police must be called to deal with the situation. However staff may search pupils' lockers or desks if they believe that drugs are stored there.

Government guidelines encourage schools to deal with cases individually and to take into account the circumstances surrounding each incident. Schools are almost always expected to tell parents of their child's involvement with illegal drugs.

Schools have a legal duty to inform the police where they believe or suspect a pupil to be in possession of a controlled drug. Pupils in possession of substances that are not controlled, e.g. alcohol, solvents, tobacco, should be dealt with under the school's disciplinary procedures. Schools must make a full record of every incident involving unauthorised drugs and contact the pupil's parents/guardian. The police should not interview anyone under the age of 18 without a parent, adult friend, or social worker being present.

Any pupil who has been involved with unauthorised drugs at school runs the risk of being excluded – either for a fixed period, or permanently. However, exclusion from school should not be automatic. The schools should first look for other ways of dealing with the pupil's behaviour and exclusion should normally take place only after a thorough investigation or when there is an immediate threat to the safety of other pupils in the school.

use the law with care try talking first

A pupil who breaks an important school rule or who persistently breaks minor school rules can be excluded from school. A Principal of a school may suspend a pupil for up to five days but if the Principal wishes to extend the suspension beyond this he or she must seek the approval of the chair of the board of governors of the school. Guidance from the Department of Education indicates that a decision to exclude a pupil should be exceptional. Truancy, lateness, forgetting homework, or pregnancy are not reasons for exclusion.

A suspension may not last longer than 45 days in a school year. When a school decides to suspend a pupil they must inform the pupil's parents in writing, explaining the reasons for the suspension, how long it will last for. They must invite the parents in to school to discuss the suspension. If the school does not follow the correct procedures or if the suspension is unreasonable in the circumstances then it may be open to legal challenge by way of Judicial Review.

If a school decides to expel a pupil then the parents must be invited to a meeting with the chair of the board of governors, a representative of the Education and Library Board and the Principal to discuss the proposed expulsion. Parents must also be informed in writing about the right to appeal and the time limits for lodging an appeal. If the parents disagree with the decision then they can appeal to an independent tribunal. Only the parents can appeal, the pupil cannot appeal unless they are aged 18 or over.

The Department of Education publication 'Promoting Positive Behaviour' is useful and the Children's Law Centre produce a leaflet on suspensions and exclusions for young people. See **contacts**.

reports & records

Principals must provide information on the performance of each pupil at the end of each key stage and each year of sixth form.

Pupils in secondary schools or pupils aged over 11 in special schools can have access themselves as can their parents to formative school records. These are formal records of academic achievement and other skills, talents and abilities. The parents of pupils in primary school or pupils in special schools aged under 11 can also have access. A young person has to be 16 to get access themselves to any other educational records. The school can withhold certain items if it feels they might damage the mental or physical health of the pupil or someone else.

If a pupil is refused permission to sit a public exam, eg GCSE or A level, his or her parents may appeal to the school governors against this decision. A pupil who has been entered for an exam but fails to sit it, without good reason, can be asked to pay the entry fee.

If a candidate does not do as well as expected in an exam, the school can ask for their paper to be checked, to make sure that the marks have been correctly assessed. Schools can also ask for a re-mark if it's felt that a serious mistake has been made in marking the paper. If they still remain dissatisfied, the school can lodge an appeal with the examining board and then the Council for the Curriculum Examinations and Assessment. It is possible that compensation may be awarded if an examining board makes a serious error and this causes the student, for example, to lose their university place.

There is very little that can be done for a candidate who does badly in an exam because of poor teaching or a failure by a teacher to follow the correct procedure - or even the right syllabus. The examining board give grades based on the candidate's actual performance. Action through the courts for compensation would be extremely costly with no guarantee of success.

bullying

Schools have a legal duty to make sure students are safe in school, including on their journey to and from school. All schools must have an anti-bullying policy and policies protecting students from racial or sexual discrimination, and must act immediately on any evidence of a pupil being bullied. If they do not, they may be sued for negligence.

Schools are entitled to exclude pupils permanently who are persistent bullies and in serious cases may inform the police.

Childline provides a 24-hour telephone helpline, with trained counsellors able to talk to children and young people about bullying, tel 0800 1111.

Safety

Schools have a legal duty to safeguard and promote the welfare of children at all times when they are at school or when they are in the lawful control or charge of the teaching staff of the school, for example on a school trip. If the action of teachers is called into question, the courts will look to the standard of care provided and decide whether a teacher or teachers has been negligent.

■ BRIEF CASE: Bullying

Ten pupils, who bullied younger children at a school in Doncaster, were found guilty of a total of 39 charges - including blackmail, robbery, and assault. The three most prominent members of the gang were sentenced to four, six and eight months in a young offender institution.

work

and training

young citizen's **passport**

INDIVIDUALS ENGAGING IN SOCIETY

Citizenship Foundation

part-time work

The law controlling the work of young people below school leaving age is set out in the *Children (NI) Order 1995*. This states the kind of work that a young person may, or may not, do. In general, this means light work only, and may involve making deliveries, work in offices, shops, hotels or catering, or light farm or garden work for parents. The work must not be harmful or interfere with attendance at school, and a young person must have their parent's written permission to do their job.

Young people below school leaving age are not allowed to work for more than an hour before school and must have at least a half-hour break before school starts. If working during July and August, they must have a two week holiday in one block. If working outside, suitable protective clothing must be provided.

If you are under 15 you may not work for more than five hours on a Saturday or non school day, or for more than 27 hours per week. You should get one hour for meals and a break every three hours (four hours on a Saturday). If you are 15 you may not work for more than seven hours on a Saturday or non school day, or for more than 37 hours per week. You should get one hour for meals and a break every four hours.

No young person below school leaving age may be employed before 7am or after 7pm, before the end of school hours on a school day, or for more than two hours on a school day, or on a Sunday.

There are fewer restrictions on the employment of 16 or 17 year olds. However, you must not work for more than eight hours per day or 40 hours per week. People under 18 cannot normally work in a bar, unless they work in a restaurant where drinks are served with meals, or are being trained for the licensing trade under an approved training scheme.

■ BRIEF CASE

A boy of 14, working in a factory making beds, suffered severe injuries when his arm was trapped in an unguarded machine. A court fined his employer £1,000 for failing to fit a guard to the machine and £200 for employing a child. The employer also paid £438 towards the costs of the case.

Employment rights

In 1994, senior judges decided that UK laws unfairly discriminated against part-time workers. As a result, many of the rights of those in part-time jobs (even if it's for only a couple of hours per week) are now the same as those of people in full-time employment.

If you are in part-time work you...

- are protected by the anti-discrimination laws, regardless of how many hours you work or how long you have worked for your employer;
- have the right, if you have worked for your employer for one month, to be given notice if asked to leave and, after two months to receive the terms and conditions of your job, in writing;
- are entitled to redundancy pay if you are made redundant and have worked for your employer for at least two years from the age of 18; and
- are entitled to claim for unfair dismissal if you have worked for your employer for at least a year, and feel you have been unfairly sacked.

The *Part-time Workers (Prevention of Less Favourable Treatment) Regulations (NI) 2000* state that part-timers must receive the same treatment as full-time workers in relation to their hourly rates of pay, training, holiday, and maternity rights, etc.

training

Jobskills

The Jobskills Programme guarantees a training place to all 16 and 17 year olds who are no longer in full-time education. Places are available regardless of gender, marital status, sexual orientation, community background, race or disability. Trainees with a disability can enter the Programme up until their 22nd birthday. Some trainee and apprenticeship places are also available to people aged between between 18 and 24.

The Jobskills Programme offers three different training routes.

- **Jobskills Access** is for young people who are not yet ready to begin NVQ level 2 training.
- **Traineeships** provide an opportunity to gain job-related skills and NVQs at level 2. Trainees follow an agreed training plan, which lasts for up to 18 months. Traineeships can lead to more advanced qualifications, such as Modern Apprenticeship.
- **Modern Apprenticeships** are designed to prepare you for a skilled job in a particular industry. They offer on-the-job training, with pay, leading to a nationally recognised qualification. They can also provide the opportunity to go on to take a degree.

A modern apprenticeship will normally last for about three years, although this varies according to the young person's needs and their rate of progress.

For more information on training opportunities, see the Careers Service NI website, **www.careersserviceni.com**

Pay

You may be taken on as a work-based trainee or an employee. If you are a trainee, you will receive a training allowance. As an employee, you will receive at least the minimum wage - see page 38. Apprentices aged 16-18 do not qualify for the minimum wage but it is payable to those aged 19 and over after the first twelve months of their apprenticeship.

Terms and conditions

Whether you are a work-based trainee or an employee, you are entitled to receive written details of the terms and conditions of your training. If you are employed, you are covered by all the other rights and benefits mentioned in this chapter.

You must also be given an individual training plan that will explain:

- **how your training will be organised;**
- **the date when your programme begins and ends;**
- **your hours of work (if you are not employed, the maximum is 40 hours per week);**
- **details of the NVQ for which you are training.**

Problems

If you are unhappy with your training provision, you may be able to transfer to a different employer, occupational area or training organisation. Any problems should be discussed initially with the supervisor in your workplace. If your training organisation cannot finish your training, you should be given the opportunity to transfer to another training organisation with a similar training programme.

If you are absent for more than the period specified in your terms and conditions, without permission from your training organisation or employer, your training programme will end.

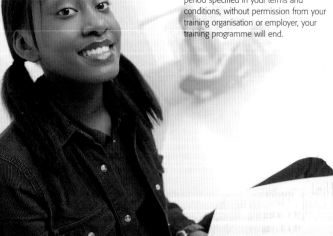

use the law with care try talking first

BRIEF CASE: Karen

Karen applied for an apprenticeship at a garage in Surrey. She was the best qualified applicant and had already worked in a garage as part of her work experience. At her interview she was asked whether she minded spending all day in a pair of dirty overalls, covered in oil and grease. Karen said she wasn't bothered, but didn't get the job. Karen believed she had been unfairly discriminated against and took her case to an employment tribunal. The tribunal agreed and awarded just over £24,000 for loss of earnings and injury to her feelings.

You may also ask to talk to a careers adviser in your local JobCentre/Jobs and Benefits Office.

Trainees who are not in full-time employment are not entitled to a period of notice if they are dismissed from the Programme; nor can they take their case to an industrial tribunal. However, they may appeal to the training organisation. If they leave to take up the offer of another job, they do not need to work out their notice before leaving.

Employed trainees or apprentices have the same legal protection as other employees and are required to give the period of notice specified in their contract of employment.

More information is available from your local JobCentre or Jobs and Benefits Office.

Equal opportunities

Trainees have the same protection as employees against unfair discrimination. Help is available from your local JobCentre/Jobs and Benefits Office and Citizens Advice Bureau. For more information, see **equal rights**, page 41.

Health & safety

Your training organisation and employer must make sure that the place where you train is safe. You have a legal responsibility to follow all safety procedures and use equipment in the way instructed.

If you have an accident, or are worried about safety, speak to your supervisor immediately. If you are injured or become ill while training, you should also contact your local JobCentre Jobs and Benefits Office. You should continue to receive your training allowance for three weeks after an accident and then you will need to make a claim for Income Support.

Anyone injured on a government funded training scheme may be able to claim Disablement Benefit. Contact your local JobCentre Jobs and Benefits Office for details.

training

New Deal is designed to help unemployed people find work by providing advice and support from a New Deal Personal Adviser, together with opportunities for training and work experience. The New Deal for 18 to 24 year olds is for young people in this age group who have been claiming Jobseeker's Allowance for six months or more. New Deal 25+ is for those aged 25 or over who have been claiming Jobseeker's Allowance for eighteen months or more. Both New Deal programmes offer early entry to certain groups of people such as lone parents, those with a health condition or disability, ex-offenders, homeless people etc who might find it difficult to get work without the additional help offered by New Deal.

The New Deal programmes are compulsory in the sense that someone who does not take part without good reason stands to lose their Jobseeker's Allowance.

If you are eligible you will be asked to attend an interview with a New Deal Personal Adviser who will explain the programme, help you to draw up an action plan to find work, give you advice and monitor progress through a series of fortnightly interviews. If, at the end of this initial period (known as the Gateway, which may last for up to four months) you have not found work you will be required to attend a New Deal option full-time for up to six months. The New Deal for 18 to 24 year olds has four options – work experience with a voluntary sector organisation or environmental organisation, training with a work placement or a subsidised job with an employer. Your Personal Adviser will help you to select which option offers you the best opportunity of getting permanent work.

Again, if you do not agree to start or attend your option, or fail to turn up for interviews with your Personal Adviser without giving a good reason, payment of your Jobseeker's Allowance is at risk of being stopped.

Young people on the work experience/training options receive either a wage or an allowance equal to their former rate of Jobseeker's Allowance plus £15.38 per week. Those receiving an allowance continue to be entitled to other benefits such as housing benefit and prescriptions.

More information is available at your local JobCentre or Jobs and Benefits office.

applying for work

Applications

Read through the application form before starting to fill it in. Draft your longer answers in rough, until you are happy with what you have written.

All the information you give should be correct. An employer is entitled to dismiss someone who is deliberately misleading on their application form or at interview.

Your CV

Some adverts for jobs tell you to send for an application form, others will ask for a letter with your curriculum vitae, usually known as a C.V. This is something that you write or type, giving personal details, qualifications, experience, and interests. Make several copies and don't forget to keep one yourself.

use the law with care try talking first

Referees

You will need the names of two people who are prepared to act as your referees, to write a short report or reference about you for an employer. One referee is usually your last employer, or the head teacher or year tutor in your school.

Interviews

If you've not been to the office or building before, leave yourself extra time to find it; or go round and find out where it is beforehand. If you can't make the appointment, phone or write to explain and ask for a more convenient time.

Have a few questions ready to ask - about what the course or job involves. If they offer you a place or job, before you accept try to think if there's anything else you need to know. If there is, ask.

Everyone at work has a contract - whether full or part-time, permanent or fixed term.

A contract is another word for the agreement between you and your employer, spelling out the arrangements that will affect your work - such as pay, hours, the sort of job you will do, holidays and the notice you have to give, or you can expect to receive, when your employment comes to an end.

Terms and conditions in writing

If you are to be employed for more than one month, your employer must give you a written statement within two months of starting work, setting out the terms and conditions of your job.

This statement should give...

- **your job title and place of work;**
- **your starting date;**
- **your rate of pay, and details of how and when you will be paid;**
- **your hours of work;**
- **your holidays and holiday pay;**
- **arrangements for sick pay and pension;**
- **details of the firm's disciplinary procedures (only if 20 or more people are employed), and how complaints at work are dealt with; and**
- **the amount of notice that you or your employer must give if your contract is to be ended.**

contracts

People often think that contracts have to be written down - they don't. They can be agreed verbally - but it's a good idea to have things in writing, in case there's disagreement about what you're expected to do.

Check your contract carefully. Make sure you agree with what it says and that it covers everything you are being asked to do. If it is different from the agreement made at your interview, point this out. Keep safe all pay slips, letters and papers you are given by your employer.

Take care

If you agree to do something on a regular basis that is not written into your contract - like working on a Saturday - you may be, in law, agreeing to a new term or condition of work. If you decide later that working every Saturday is not a good idea, your boss may be entitled to insist that you continue. By turning up for work six days a week, you may have actually changed your contract by your conduct.

Pay

Your wages will either be agreed between you and your boss or else based on rates agreed between employers and the trade union. Either way, your employer must give you a detailed written pay statement each time you are paid, showing exactly what you are being paid and how much is being taken off in tax, national insurance etc. It is up to your employer to choose how you are paid. This can be by cash, cheque, or straight into your bank account.

Your rate of sick pay must be explained in your contract. It will probably say either that you will be paid at your standard rate for a certain length of time, or that you will be given statutory sick pay. This is set each year and is usually lower than your normal pay. If you are off sick for four or more days in a row (including Sundays and bank holidays) you will receive statutory sick pay from your employer for up to 28 weeks. You don't have to claim statutory sick pay, just follow your employer's rules for notifying sickness.

You can check what you should receive in leaflets available from Social Security Agency offices and libraries.

MINIMUM PAY

Under the *National Minimum Wage Act 1998*, from October 2006, the minimum wage payable to 16 and 17 year olds who are above compulsory school leaving age should be £3.30 per hour. For people aged 18 – 21 it will be £4.45 per hour, and £5.35 for people aged 22 and over.

For more details, phone the Minimum Wage Helpline, tel 0845 6500 207.

use the law with care try talking first

Hours

Your hours of work will normally be agreed between you and your employer, although there are some jobs where these are limited by law for reasons of health and safety.

Workers who are 18 or under may not work more than eight hours a day or 40 hours a week. Nor may they ordinarily work between 10pm and 6am. Some night work is allowed in certain jobs, such as the armed forces, farm work, catering, working in a pub, restaurant or hotel, working in a bakery, newspaper delivery and retail trading. However an adult must supervise the work and rest periods must be given.

The *Working Time Regulations* set a maximum working week of 48 hours, including overtime, calculated over 17 weeks for workers aged 19 and over. You can agree to do more than this, but your employer cannot pressurise you to do so. You are also entitled to:

- **a rest break of 20 minutes when you work for more than six hours at a time (or 30 minutes every four hours if you are under 18);**

HOLIDAYS

The *Working Time Regulations* give most people over 16 the right to at least four weeks' paid holiday a year. During the first year of employment, you have the right to take one twelfth of your annual holiday entitlement for each month worked. Some jobs are not covered by the Regulations, for example those in the transport and fishing industries, the police, and armed forces.

- **at least 11 consecutive hours off in any 24 hour period (12 hours off, if you are under 18).**
- **Workers who believe that the hours they are expected to work do not follow the regulations, can take their case to an employment tribunal.**

health & safety

Safety

Employers have a legal duty to take care of the safety of their staff. If they don't, they are breaking the *Health and Safety at Work (NI) Order 1978*.

This means that the equipment that you use must not be dangerous or defective, and that the people you work with must work safely and responsibly.

Your duty is to follow safety regulations and to take care of your own and other people's safety.

Your boss must give you details of the health and safety arrangements in writing.

If you are worried about health and safety, raise the matter with your supervisor. Your employer may not dismiss you or treat you unfairly for raising genuine concerns, as long as you follow the right procedures. If you remain concerned, contact the local offices of the Health and Safety Executive for Northern Ireland. Your local Citizens Advice Bureau will be able to tell you how to do this or see **contacts**.

health & safety

■ BRIEF CASE: Irene

Irene worked as a secretary in an office where several people smoked. Although a nonsmoker herself, she felt no ill effects as the area was well ventilated. However, when Irene's section was moved to another part of the building, with poorer ventilation, the smoke and smell started to become a problem. Despite Irene's complaints, her employer did nothing to discourage people from smoking or to create a better working environment. After nearly three years, Irene left the firm and found another job, but decided to take her case to an employment tribunal to claim unfair dismissal, saying she had been forced to leave because of her uncomfortable working conditions. The tribunal agreed - an employer has a duty to provide a working environment that is suitable for employees to work in.

Accidents	If you are injured at work, report the matter to your supervisor straightaway and, unless the injury is very small, see a doctor. Make a note of what happened, check to see whether you are entitled to any welfare benefits and get legal advice from either your trade union or a solicitor. You may be entitled to compensation for your injuries.
Using a computer screen	If you have a problem with your eyes that you think might be due to using display screen equipment at work, your employer has a duty to arrange for you to have an eyesight test if you ask for one, and to do whatever they reasonably can at work to reduce further problems. This is all part of a general requirement for employers to check on the health and safety risks to people using computer screens at work, contained in the *Health and Safety (Display Screen Equipment) Regulations (NI) 1992*.

■ BRIEF CASE: Gary

Gary, 18, worked in a butcher's and was cutting meat when his hand slipped and he cut off the top of two fingers. His boss had often told him to use a special guard - but most people at work ignored this, so Gary didn't bother either. Gary was awarded damages in court because his employer did not make sure that he was working in the right way, but they were reduced by a third because he hadn't followed the safety instructions.

use the law with care **try talking first**

Discrimination

It is against the law for an employer or training organisations to discriminate against someone because of their religion, race, colour, country of origin, nationality, ethnic group, sex, marital status, disability, political opinion, sexual orientation or because they work part-time. See also page 42.

This is explained in a number of laws and regulations including the *Equal Pay Act (NI) 1970 (amended 1984), Sex Discrimination (NI) Order 1976 (amended 1988), Race Relations (NI) Order 1997, Disability Discrimination Act 1995, Fair Employment and Treatment (NI) Order 1998, Northern Ireland Act 1998, Equality (Disability etc) (NI) Order 2000* and the *Employment Equality (Sexual Orientation) Regulations (NI) 2003.*

A few jobs are excluded from the sex discrimination laws. These include acting, modelling, sport, and jobs involving physical or close contact with the opposite sex.

Direct & indirect discrimination

Not treating a person as well as someone else because of their skin colour, sex etc is called **direct discrimination**.

Indirect discrimination is more subtle, and this occurs when conditions are laid down for a job that unfairly limit the chances of people from one sex, or a particular ethnic group. Both are unlawful.

Disability

The *Disability Discrimination Act 1995* protects certain groups of disabled people from unfair discrimination.

It is against the law to treat a person with a disability less favourably than someone without, unless it can be justified for a reason related to the disability. Employers are required to make reasonable adjustments to the working environment that would enable a person with disabilities to be employed.

■ BRIEF CASE: Eugene

**Eugene suffered constant racist taunts from other workers on the building site where he worked, and the management did little to stop it. They said that "black bastard" and "nigger" were words often used on sites. The tribunal decided that Eugene had been directly discriminated against.
He was awarded £2,000 damages.**

■ BRIEF CASE: Susan

Susan, a train driver on London Underground, was forced to hand in her notice when new shift rosters meant that it was impossible for her to work and look after her three year old child. She took her case to an employment tribunal, complaining of sex discrimination. The tribunal decided that the new working arrangements indirectly discriminated against women because more women were single parents.

Other discrimination

A wide range of legislation (see under discrimination, page 41) protects people who face discrimination at work because of their sexuality, religion or beliefs. Transsexuals (people who have changed sex) are also protected from discrimination and harassment at work. Regulations against age discrimination come into force in October 2006.

Help and advice

If you feel you have been a victim of unfair discrimination at work, you can get help from your local Citizens Advice Bureau, Law Centre or trade union. Advice and information on racial matters, sex discrimination and on disability is also available from the Equality Commission.

If you can't sort out things informally, you may be advised to take your complaint to an employment tribunal. This must be done within three months (or six months, if it is a claim under the *Equal Pay Act (NI)*). If you win, the tribunal can award damages to compensate you for the losses you have suffered. You may be able to settle your case without the need to go to court but, if not, be prepared for a long and difficult battle, and remember to take legal advice.

Sexual harassment

Sexual harassment covers a whole range of things from rude remarks to leering and unwanted physical contact. They are known in law as direct discrimination, under the *Sex Discrimination (NI) Order 1976*. Although they usually apply to women, men can be victims too.

If you can, it's often better to try to sort things out personally. But if the harassment continues, don't be afraid to complain. It's not always easy to prove in court, but judges are now prepared to award damages when the victim can show that they have suffered some disadvantage or injury to their feelings from the sexual harassment.

■ BRIEF CASE

An employment tribunal decided that a secretary, who was sacked when she complained about being groped by a senior member of staff at a Christmas party, was unfairly dismissed. She was awarded £4,700 in damages.

use the law with care **try talking first**

maternity & family rights

Maternity rights

All women at work who are expecting a baby have certain minimum legal rights. Some employers provide more than these. You can check your position from your contract.

Time off with pay for antenatal care

This applies to full and part-time workers, and it makes no difference how long you have worked for your employer. Your employer cannot insist that you make up the time, or that you take the appointment in your free time.

At least 26 weeks maternity leave

You are entitled to 26 weeks of ordinary maternity leave no matter how long you have worked for your employer, and whether you are full or part-time. An additional 26 weeks of maternity leave is available if you've worked for your employer for at least 26 weeks continuously by the fourteenth week before the child is due.

All benefits, except pay, listed in your contract, continue throughout the first 26 weeks of ordinary maternity leave – including medical insurance, pension, and even a company car, if you have one. Some benefits, such as statutory holidays, will continue throughout both the first 26 weeks of ordinary maternity leave and the 26 weeks of additional maternity leave.

Correct procedures

If you don't follow the correct procedures in applying for maternity leave, you risk losing the right to return to your job after your baby is born. For example, you must give notice to your employer by the end of the fifteenth week before the baby is due. The personnel department at work, your trade union, or local Citizens' Advice Bureau can explain what you need to do.

Maternity pay

If you have been working for your employer for long enough, you are entitled to maternity pay for the first 26 weeks of ordinary maternity leave including the time you take off before your baby is born. This will probably be lower than your usual rate, unless it says otherwise in your contract. If you are on a low income or have not worked for long enough to qualify for maternity pay, you may still be entitled to a maternity allowance from the Social Security Agency. A guide to maternity rights is available free from the Department for Employment and Learning, see **contacts**. The standard rate of maternity pay and the maternity allowance is £106 per week, or 90 per cent of your average weekly earnings, if less.

Paternity leave

If you become a father you have the right to two weeks' paid paternity leave. Paternity leave is also available if you adopt a baby or become a stepfather to a baby. As with maternity leave, you must follow the correct procedures. The personnel department at work, your trade union or local CAB can explain what you need to do.

The standard rate of paternity pay is the same as for maternity pay. A guide to paternity rights is available from the Department for Employment and Learning, see **contacts**.

Parental leave

Both parents have a right to take up to 13 weeks' unpaid parental leave over the first five years of their child's life provided they have worked for their employer for at least a year. During this time their job will be protected. The leave must be agreed with the employer. Unreasonable objections can be referred to an employment tribunal. Parents of disabled children are entitled to 18 weeks' unpaid leave over the first 18 years of the child's life.

Time off

Regardless of how long you have worked for your employer, you have the right to take unpaid time off for urgent family problems, such as an accident or sudden illness, but you must give your employer the reasons for your absence as soon as possible. You may only take a reasonable amount of time. If your employer refuses, you can complain to an industrial tribunal.

Right to request flexible working

If you have 26 weeks' service and are a parent, stepparent, adopter, foster carer or guardian of a child who is under six years old or a disabled child who is under 18 years old, you have the right to request flexible working hours. Your employer can either agree or refuse your request. If you believe that your request has been refused unreasonably then you should complain, and if your employer does not follow the correct procedure you can refer your request to a tribunal.

trade unions

Membership

It is up to you whether you join a trade union. Trade unions don't only negotiate wages for their members. They also give advice, inform members of their rights and act on their behalf over difficulties with their employer. An employer must not sack someone for either belonging or not belonging to a trade union.

Not all employers want to work with unions. But, if there are 21 or more people working for an employer, a trade union may be able to force the employer to recognise the union and to negotiate with them.

Industrial action

If you take industrial action - for example, by stopping work - you may be breaking your contract. However, if the strike has been lawfully organised and correctly balloted, your employer is not entitled to dismiss you for taking part. This is automatically unfair and you may have a case for compensation. But you cannot claim unfair dismissal if you are sacked for taking part in an unofficial strike.

If you're sacked or made redundant, your legal rights mainly depend on how long you have been working for the firm.

Notice Unless you have done something very serious and committed what's known in law as gross misconduct - such as theft or fighting - your boss should not sack you on the spot. Your contract should state the notice to which you are entitled, and this usually depends on how long you have been working for your employer.

After one month's employment, either side should give one week's notice. After two years' employment, your employer should give you two weeks' notice, three weeks' after three years, and so on, up to twelve weeks' notice for employment which has lasted twelve years or more.

However, your notice period might be longer if this is stated in your contract, and your employer may decide to pay you instead of letting you work out your notice.

Reasons in writing If you are fired by your employer, for whom you have worked for more than one year, you can ask for a written statement of the reasons for your dismissal. Your employer must provide this within 14 days.

Redundancy This happens when an employer no longer needs the job done for which you were employed. Your rights mainly depend on your age and how long you have worked for the firm.

If you are made redundant, you have a right to redundancy pay, if you:

- **have worked for your employer for a continuous period of at least two years since you were 18;**
- **are under retirement age; and**
- **have not unreasonably turned down an offer of another job from your employer.**

If your employer has gone bust, you may be able to get a redundancy payment from the Redundancy Payments Service of the Department for Employment and Learning.

If you are made redundant, get advice from your trade union, Citizens Advice Bureau or a solicitor as soon as possible. If you feel that the way you were chosen for redundancy was unfair or unreasonable, you may also be able to claim unfair dismissal.

Information You may get more information about your rights to a redundancy payment from your local JobCentre or from the Department for Employment and Learning website, **www.delni.gov.uk/er**

losing your job

UNFAIR DISMISSAL

If you feel that you have been unfairly dismissed, and have worked for your employer continuously for a year or more, you can make a complaint to an industrial tribunal.

Even if you have not been sacked, but leave your job because of the behaviour of your employer, you may have a claim for unfair dismissal. This is known in law as constructive dismissal, but will only be successful if you can show that your employer has broken your employment contract. If you are thinking of resigning because of this, keep a record of what is happening and, before you hand in your notice, write to your employer explaining your reasons for leaving.

Take legal advice before you make a claim for unfair dismissal. Your trade union, Labour Relations Agency, local Citizens Advice Bureau or a solicitor can help. If you are unhappy about your dismissal, don't delay in seeking assistance. You only have three months in which to make a complaint.

If the tribunal agrees that your dismissal was unfair, your employer will probably be ordered to pay you a sum in compensation. This is based on the amount of redundancy you would be entitled to, plus a figure for compensation. The maximum basic redundancy award is £8,700 and the maximum figure for compensation is £58,400.

There are no limits to the damages you can receive if you lose your job through disability, race, or sex discrimination or if you are dismissed unfairly or selected for redundancy for reasons connected with health and safety matters.

■ BRIEF CASE: Sacked!

Jeannette's son was ill in the night and Jeanette overslept the next morning. When she arrived late at the video rental company where she worked, she was sacked. She explained what had happened, but her boss took no notice. Jeannette took her case to an employment tribunal, who decided that she had been unfairly dismissed, as she had not been given a warning or a second chance.

■ BRIEF CASE: Redundant!

Business was bad and Dean was made redundant from his job at a petrol station. He was given £520 redundancy pay, but soon realised that his job was now being done by the boss's son. Dean hadn't been redundant at all, and so won his claim for unfair dismissal.

money

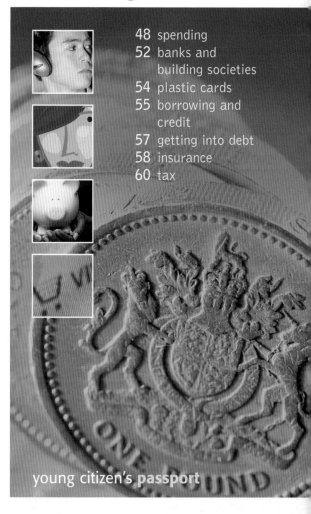

young citizen's passport

INDIVIDUALS
ENGAGING IN
SOCIETY

Citizenship Foundation

It's a contract

When you buy something from a shop or pay for a service (like a train fare or haircut) you are making an agreement, known in law as a *contract*.

The contract means that, in return for the money that you pay, the goods you buy should do everything you can reasonably expect and, in particular, all that the seller and manufacturer claim.

Once a contract has been agreed, neither side can change it on their own. Some shops allow customers to opt out of their contract by agreeing to exchange unwanted items or by providing a refund, as long as goods are returned in mint condition with the receipt. Shops don't have to do this by law, unless it was promised as part of the contract.

But what about your rights if the goods you have bought are faulty?

The Sale of Goods Act

The law applying to most everyday purchases is the *Sale of Goods Act 1979*. This was updated in 2003 to provide new protection for consumers. It says that when you buy goods from a shop or trader, they must ...

...be of satisfactory quality

This means that they must be free from faults and not scratched or damaged, and equally applies to goods bought in a sale. However, this rule does not apply if the fault was pointed out by the sales assistant or if you inspected the item and had a good opportunity to discover the fault.

Second-hand goods bought from a shop or trader must also be of satisfactory quality. This protection does not apply if you bought the goods privately (e.g. through a 'small ad') – when the buyer is responsible for deciding the quality of what she or he wants to buy.

...match the description

The goods must be the same as the description on the packaging, or advertisement or given by the assistant at the time of sale. A bracelet marked solid silver, must be just that.

This rule also applies to second-hand goods, including those sold privately.

...be fit for all their intended purposes

This means that they must do what the seller, packaging or advertisements claim. A watch sold as waterproof should not stop if you forget to take it off in the shower.

GETTING IT RIGHT

If you're buying something expensive, and want to do some research beforehand, Which? magazine, available in most libraries gives a guide to the price and performance of many products. You can also go to a shop and ask just to see an item, without buying it. If you decide to make a purchase, keep the receipt in case you have a complaint.

Services too

Dry cleaners, shoe repairers, hairdressers, travel agents and many others provide a service - and you are protected by law if that service is inadequate.

Under the *Supply of Goods and Services Act 1982*, a service must be provided...

- **with reasonable care and skill;**
- **within a reasonable time; and**
- **for a reasonable charge.**

Problems? Problems are less likely to occur if certain things are agreed before the work is started. How much will it cost? How long will it take? What happens if the work can't be finished? Try to sort these out first.

Handle your complaint just as you would if it were for faulty goods. Don't be afraid to seek advice. Help is available from your local Citizens Advice Bureau or consumer advice centre.

Some trades, such as travel agents, garages, dry cleaners, shoe sellers etc have their own associations laying down a code of practice or standards. These have no legal standing, but the associations can put pressure on their members to treat customers' complaints in a reasonable way. It may be worth a try, and your local library can give you the address to contact.

OPEN COME IN

spending

PUT DOWNS

Some businesses will do as much as they can to help you with a problem over something you have bought; others may claim that there is nothing they can do. Don't give up if the shop tries to get out of its legal obligations.

...we'll send it back to the workshop

Only if you want them to. If you act reasonably quickly you can choose whether to ask for a full or partial refund, compensation or to have the goods repaired or replaced (if that is a practical option). If the goods have developed a fault in the first six months it is assumed they were faulty when it you bought them (unless the shop can prove otherwise).

... you'll have to take it up with the manufacturer

Wrong. You bought the goods from the shop and your contract was with them, not with a manufacturer on the other side of the world. If the goods genuinely don't work, the shop has not kept its side of the contract and you have a right to your money back. Shops normally have to accept responsibility to you for the manufacturer's claims.

...we'll give you a credit note

No. If the goods are faulty, you're entitled to your money back. You don't have to accept a credit note if you don't want to. If you do accept a credit note, check where and when you can use it – some credit notes must be used within a fixed time and only in exchange for certain goods or services.

...sorry, it's out of guarantee

This can be tricky. A major problem with an expensive computer three months after the guarantee has run out means a large repair bill. Raise it with the dealer and ask to talk to the manager. Produce the documentation and use the manufacturer's literature (which probably stresses reliability and quality) to point out that it is not reasonable to expect a failure after such a short period. There's no hard and fast law about what is reasonable in terms of a product failure. It depends on the circumstances.

...we don't give refunds on sale goods

Wrong. Unless the fault was pointed out to you or was something you should have seen when you bought them, goods bought in sales carry all the protection of the *Sale of Goods Act 1979*.

...we'll give you a replacement

Only if that's what you want. However, if by now the fault has led you to decide that you don't really want the product after all, you are entitled to your money back - not a replace-ment. It's up to you to choose what to do.

50

The small claims court

If you cannot get any satisfaction over a problem with faulty goods or poor service, you can write to the person concerned warning them that you will try to recover the money they owe you by taking your case to the small claims court (strictly known as the small claims procedure). This is an informal way of settling disputes, at a fraction of the normal cost, in which a judge hears your case without the expense of lawyers. Cases usually involve claims of less than £5,000 and can be brought only by someone of 18 or over. You can get more details from your local county court (under Northern Ireland Court Services in the phone book), the Citizens Advice Bureau or a consumer advice centre, see **contacts**.

Finding it's wrong

If you are not satisfied with something that you have bought....

> **Stop using it straightaway and take it back, with the receipt and guarantee (if you have one), to the shop where you bought it. It strengthens your case if you can do this as soon as possible. Your contract was with the shop, not the manufacturer, so it is the shop's responsibility to deal with your complaint. Even if you have lost the receipt, the contract still exists.**

> **Before you take the goods back, decide what you are going to say and what you would like the shop to do. Do you want your money back, or will you accept a repair or a replacement item?**

> **Think about your legal position. A faulty stop button on a personal stereo means that it is not of satisfactory quality. Don't be afraid to use the law when making your case.**

> **If the shop assistant doesn't help, ask for someone more senior.**

> **If you bought the goods by mail order or from a shop some distance away, it's easier to telephone or write. Keep a copy of all letters, send a photocopy of your receipt (keep the original), and if you talk on the phone get the name of the person you spoke to. Make a brief note of the conversation.**

Buying over the phone or on the Internet

The same rules apply as when you buy from a shop but the trader must give you some basic information like the name and address of the person you are dealing with and, in most cases, you should be given the chance to cancel your order within seven days.

You can get more details from the General Consumer Council for Northern Ireland or a Citizens Advice Bureau, see **contacts**.

A regular bank account is normally only available if you are 18 or over (or are 16 or 17 with a steady income or there is an adult who will act as your guarantor). A basic or starter account may be available from 16.

WHY HAVE AN ACCOUNT?

- many employers insist on paying salary or wages directly into an account;
- an account is needed for a student loan;
- the money can earn interest;
- regular accounts come with a cheque book and plastic card to pay for things;
- you can pay cheques other people give you into an account.

CHOOSING A BANK OR BUILDING SOCIETY

You will probably want to know:
- whether it has a branch near you and offers on-line banking;
- whether there are convenient cash points;
- the services offered and the charges;
- the level of interest paid on the money you have in the account. There will be leaflets on this, or you can ask a member of staff; and,
- its special offers for young people. But don't be persuaded by offers of free gifts if the services and charges are unattractive compared with other banks or building societies.

What types of accounts are there?

The two main types are current accounts and savings accounts.

Current accounts

A current account is the normal account for day-to-day transactions. You pay in the money you receive, such as your wages, salary or student loan.

If you are 18 or over, you can usually get a chequebook and a cheque guarantee card so that you can pay for things by giving a signed cheque. You may also be given one or more plastic cards. These are described on page 54. You'll receive a regular bank statement – probably once a month – to show you how much has been paid in, how much you have withdrawn and your balance.

Using a cheque book and guarantee card

A chequebook contains a number of cheques with your name on. The person you give a cheque to pays it into their bank account, and after a few days the money is taken (debited) from your account and added (credited) to the other person's account.

If you haven't got enough money in your current account to cover the value of the cheque you have written, the bank may refuse to honour your cheque and it will bounce.

You may also be issued with a cheque guarantee card. This enables you to pay for things more easily, as it guarantees that the bank will honour

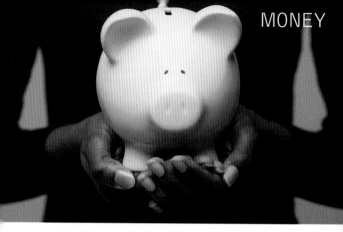

your cheque up to the amount stated on the card – usually £50 or £100. If there isn't enough money in your account to cover the value of the cheques you have written with your cheque guarantee card, you'll go overdrawn and may have to pay bank charges and interest. Strictly speaking it is an offence to write a cheque when you know there is not enough money in your account to cover it, unless you already have the permission of your bank to do so, see page 55. Don't keep your chequebook and guarantee card together.

What do I do if someone gives me a cheque? When someone pays you by cheque, look to see that is correctly written out, that it is for the right amount, that it has been signed, and that it is not "post-dated" (one with a future date on).

As soon as possible pay the cheque into your current account using a paying in slip. Cheques that are more than six months old may not be accepted.

Savings accounts A savings account provides a higher rate of interest. Most do not come with a chequebook or plastic card, and some have restrictions on when you can withdraw your money. However, you will still be able to withdraw money if you really have to, but will probably lose some of the extra interest.

If you keep money in your savings account at the same time as being overdrawn on your current account or having a loan, you may find the interest you pay on your overdraft or loan is higher than the interest you earn on your savings account - so you will be worse off.

What about tax on the interest I earn? Interest earned on bank and building society accounts is usually paid after tax has been deducted from it. Unless you have a high income, that is normally the end of the matter, and there is no more tax to pay; see **tax** page 60. If you are not a taxpayer - because your earnings are not high enough - you can either get the tax back by contacting a tax office or you can choose to have the interest paid to you without deduction of the tax. Your bank or building society will have the forms for you to complete that allow them to do this.

FAULTY GOODS

What about plastic cards?

Plastic cards can be extremely useful. But they can cause difficulties if you are not careful how you use them. You usually have to be 18 to get one. There are many types of card with different functions:

- **Cheque guarantee card** - See page 52. This guarantees that the bank will honour your cheque.

- **Cash card** - This lets you make withdrawals from cash machines. You will be given a confidential personal identity number - PIN - to use with your card. It is essential that no one else knows your PIN. Never keep a record of it with your card. If you do, anyone stealing it can immediately get at your cash.

- **Debit card e.g. Maestro** - This card allows you to buy things without writing a cheque or using cash. You can also use it to pay for goods over the telephone or on the Internet. Your account is automatically debited with the amount you have spent. You can only go overdrawn with a debit card, if you have the bank's agreement.

- **Credit card e.g. Mastercard and Visa** - Like a debit card, holding a credit card allows people to purchase goods and services from a huge range of shops and other suppliers, including over the telephone or on the Internet. A credit card, however, allows the shop to be paid now but the customer does not receive the bill until later.

The firm issuing the credit card is, in effect, lending the customer the money to buy things. The bank will check out their customers' credit worthiness. They may charge a yearly fee for the card. When a credit card account is opened a spending limit is set. If this is broken, the card may be cancelled.

LOSING YOUR CARDS

If you lose a card or your chequebook, notify the card company or bank immediately. They can often be contacted 24 hours a day. If your card is lost or stolen and used by someone else before you have reported the loss you may have to pay the first £50 of any debts incurred.

Each month a statement is sent to the customer, showing what has been spent using the card, how much is owed, and what minimum payment must be made. Cardholders who do not pay off their bill in full are charged a high rate of interest.

Customers can compare the costs of different cards by looking at the Annual Percentage Rate (APR). The APR is the rate of interest charged by the firm issuing the credit card. All organisations issuing cards have to quote their APR, which shows the total cost of the credit. A credit card with a high APR costs more than one with a low APR.

- **Store card** - These are credit cards issued by stores, for example department stores or sports shops. You open an account with the store that in effect lends you money to buy their goods or services.

They will send you a regular statement showing how much you have spent, and how much you owe them. With some cards, you have to pay off the full amount each month. With others, you may be able to pay a fixed minimum amount each time; the rest will be carried forward and appear on your next statement.

You will have to pay interest on the amount you haven't paid off. These interest charges can be high. You can check the APR and compare it with your credit card.

- **Chip & PIN** - This has been introduced to cut down on fraud. Instead of signing a paper receipt, you enter a four-digit PIN, just like you do at a cash machine.

borrowing and credit

Borrowing from a bank or building society

A bank or building society lends money either through allowing an overdraft or by making a loan.

Overdrafts

A person becomes overdrawn when they spend more money than they have in their bank account. The most expensive overdraft is an unauthorised one - which is run up without the agreement of the bank. Interest is paid on the amount overdrawn, and charges are added on top.

If you ever find yourself in this situation, it is important to get in touch with the bank soon as you can.

If you need to go overdrawn, you can usually arrange with your bank an authorised overdraft, up to an agreed amount. Interest may be charged. Students may be offered interest-free overdrafts.

borrowing and credit

LOANS

A loan is an arrangement with your bank - or other financial institution - under which you are lent a specific amount of money. You enter into a contract for the loan. This will be for a set period, with an agreed rate of interest and time over which you have to repay the full amount. If you are under 18 it is very unlikely that you will be able to get a bank loan, as contracts with "minors" are not usually binding so the bank will be taking too big a risk.

A loan is usually a better way of borrowing money than running up large debts on a credit card, but it is important to check that the repayment terms are affordable.

Buying goods by instalments - credit or hire purchase

You can often buy more expensive goods (cars, computers, TVs) by instalment - that is, by paying only part of the price at the time of purchase, and paying the rest later. This is known as buying on credit or on "tick." Sometimes credit is available interest-free, but credit is normally an expensive way of paying for things. It is always a good idea to check the charges (the APR) that are being made .

Hire purchase is a special form of buying on credit. Technically the shop sells the goods to a finance company and you pay to "hire" them over an agreed period. When you have paid off what you owe you make a small final payment to purchase the goods (hence "hire purchase"). Only then do you become the owner.

Second thoughts If you signed a credit deal at home (or away from the shop or business premises) you have a right to cancel if you act quickly. You will be sent a second copy of the agreement that will tell you how to cancel if you want to. If you signed the agreement on business premises then it's much harder to cancel unless the form has to be sent away to the credit company for its signature. Then you can withdraw as long as you tell them before they have signed up.

use the law with care try talking first

getting into debt

People get into debt for all sorts of reasons, often through no fault of their own. They may find they owe money to several different people and are tempted to borrow more to pay off some of these debts. This often becomes even more expensive.

You know it's getting serious when you start getting badgered to make repayments by the people you owe money to - your "creditors" - and you can't meet all the demands.

What to do

- **Don't ignore the problem:** it won't go away and will get worse the longer you leave it. You can get help and, in most cases, you can take control.
- **Draw up a budget:** list all the money you owe and the people to whom it is owed; what your income and reasonable living expenses are; and see how much you can afford to pay back.
- **List your debts in their order of priority:** at the top are those where non payment can have really serious consequences - like losing your flat or home; having the electricity or gas cut off, or where non payment is a criminal offence (like council tax and your TV licence). You should aim to pay these off first and then work out what's left over for the others, treating them equally.
- **Contact all your creditors:** go and see them or write or phone; explain the position and show them your budget. Discuss with them what you can reasonably pay. Usually they will be prepared to negotiate an agreement with you as this improves their chances of getting paid. You may be able to agree to pay by instalments or, for a period of time, just to pay off the interest on your loan.
- **Don't borrow more without getting advice:** there are lots of people prepared to lend you more to pay off earlier debts. They are sometimes called loan-sharks. They will probably charge very high rates of interest making it even more difficult for you to get out of debt. They won't be nearly as easy to deal with if you can't keep up your repayments.

HELP

You can get help and advice from experts. Try the NI Debtline or a Citizens Advice Bureau, see contacts.

Insurance is a way of protecting yourself and your property from an unexpected loss or mishap. You can insure yourself against almost anything - losing your possessions in a fire, having them stolen or damaged, or having to face unexpected medical bills on holiday abroad. If you drive a car or motorcycle, you must be insured by law, see travel and transport, page 97 .

In return for a premium - an agreed amount of money you pay each month or year - an insurance company will, if the worst does happen, pay you compensation for the losses or damage that you insured against.

Buying insurance

There are two ways of obtaining insurance. You can either deal directly with the company, or go to a broker.

Most large insurance companies have offices in the major towns and cities. Their numbers are in the Yellow Pages or local phone book. You can often deal directly with them and arrange

your insurance cover by phone. Insurance brokers are agents who can help you choose an insurer and arrange the policy for you. They don't usually charge you for this, but instead make their money from the insurance company that you have decided to use.

All the information you give should be as accurate as possible. Questions must be answered truthfully, and any other information that could be relevant should also be given. If it's not, the insurance policy will be invalid.

Keep a copy of any form that you complete, and when you renew your insurance (usually done each year) don't forget to tell the insurance company about anything that has changed that might affect your insurance position. If you don't, your policy may be invalid.

Broker

An agent who can help you choose and apply for insurance.

Cover

Insurance against loss or damage.

Cover note

A temporary document showing that you have insurance cover, usually sent out while the official certificate is being prepared.

Excess

The amount you will have to pay towards the cost of your claim.

No claims bonus

The discount you are given on your premium if you haven't made a claim.

Policy

The document setting out the terms and conditions of your insurance.

Premium

The amount you pay for your insurance.

Quotation

A statement of the amount you will have to pay for the insurance you asked for. You can sometimes pay an extra premium to reduce this – called a waiver.

Income Tax

Money paid in income tax is used to pay for services provided by the state - such as health, education, defence etc. Everyone who earns or receives income over a certain amount in a year pays income tax and, generally speaking, the more you earn, the more you pay. Current tax rates range from 10% – 40%. As well as earnings from full and part-time work, tips and bonuses, tax is also paid on interest from savings with banks, building societies and some National Savings accounts, on Income Support and on profits from a business and dividends from shares.

PAYE

Your employer will usually take the tax from your earnings each time you are paid and pass the money on to the tax authorities, called the Inland Revenue. Everyone is entitled to receive a certain amount of money on which they pay no tax at all. This is called a personal allowance, which, for a single person in 2005/2006, is £4,895. Income tax is paid only when your income rises above this. There are other allowances which may be available, eg for the cost of tools or special clothing if they are not provided by your employer. If you are on a training programme, your grant in most cases is not taxable.

Part-time workers should not have tax deducted from their pay, unless their income is above £94 a week. If you are a student with a holiday job, ask your employer for a form P38(S) if you think your total taxable income for the year (including earnings and income support), will be less than the basic personal allowance, i.e. £4,895. Fill in the form, return it to your employer, and you should then be paid without tax being deducted.

If you have been working and paying tax, but believe your total income for the year will be less than £4,895 ask for form P50 from your local tax office, and return it completed with your P45 from your employer. You should then receive a refund. The Inland Revenue publishes free booklets on tax, obtainable from your library or nearest tax office (under Inland Revenue in the phone book). The Taxpayer's Charter outlines the service you are entitled to expect from staff at the Inland Revenue.

Failure to complete your tax forms correctly can mean extra interest payments and even fines. The Inland Revenue runs a telephone helpline, giving information and advice on tax, see **contacts**.

Tax credits

Working Tax Credits and Child Tax Credits are available to those on low incomes to top up earnings.

BENEFITS

You may be entitled to Income Support, Jobseeker's Allowance, Maternity Allowance, a disability allowance or other social security benefits. Benefit rates normally change once a year, in April. Leaflets explaining this are available from Social Security and Jobs and Benefits offices, and sometimes local libraries and post offices. A freephone benefits information and advice line is available on 0800 220 674.

family

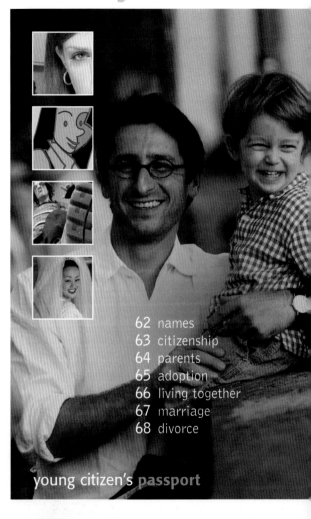

young citizen's passport

INDIVIDUALS ENGAGING IN SOCIETY

Citizenship Foundation

Within 42 days of birth, the birth and name of a child must be registered with the District Registrar of Births, Marriages and Deaths. The birth may be registered either in the district in which it took place or in which the mother lives.

The birth can be registered by either parent if they are married, but only by the mother if they are not. If unmarried parents want both their names to appear on their child's birth certificate, then they must both be present when the child is registered. The father's name can also be registered later.

Changing your name

Under 18 A child's name can be changed with the agreement of both parents, unless the child is in care or a ward of court. In this case the child's name cannot be changed without the agreement of the court or everyone with responsibility for the child. The child can also object by applying to court.

If a parent wants to change their child's name, but the other parent or the child objects - then the parent or the child can apply for a court order to prevent this. Courts are very reluctant to agree to change a child's name against their will because of the importance of a name to a child's sense of identity.

If you wish to change your name you will need your parents' agreement or a court order. If you are over 16 you can change your name by deed poll and register it at court. If your parents object, you may need a court order to override their objection.

Over 18 You can call yourself what you like and, if you want to change your name, you can just go ahead and do it. If you are married, you will usually need the agreement of your spouse. But you can't change your name to mislead or defraud someone.

Although you are free to be known by whatever name you wish, it can be difficult to prove your identity if the name you use is not the same as the one on your birth certificate. The best way to confirm your new name is by a change of name deed poll, which is a statement announcing your new name, witnessed by a solicitor. Your local Citizens Advice Bureau or a solicitor can give you more information on this.

If you marry

Women have the right to change their surname when they marry - but they don't have to. A woman can keep her own family name, or make a new one by joining her name with that of her husband. A new surname becomes official by signing the marriage register or a deed poll.

A man can change his name to that of his wife upon marriage with her consent and by using a deed poll.

CITIZENSHIP

Most of our legal rights and responsibilities arise just because we are living, working, studying etc. in a particular place - in our case, Northern Ireland. This is citizenship in its widest sense.

Sometimes, however, people need to know which country they are legally connected to (or what their nationality is). Countries can base their rules on a number of questions, such as where the person was born, how long they have lived in the country and where their parents were born or live.

In brief Currently anyone born on the island of Ireland is entitled to Irish citizenship. If either of your parents was born in Ireland or if one of your grandparents was born in Ireland you can apply for Irish citizenship.

Anyone born in the United Kingdom - including Northern Ireland - before 1 January 1983 is entitled to British citizenship. If you were born in the UK on or after this date, you are a British citizen by birth if either of your parents are British citizens or they are entitled to live here permanently. If your parents are not married, only your mother's position counts.

Becoming a British or Irish citizen by naturalisation or registration depends on a number of different factors, such as if you marry a British or Irish citizen, how long you have lived here, if you are permanently settled here (or intend to remain here permanently) and if you are of 'good character'.

This is a complicated process and you may need specialist advice. Your local Citizens Advice Bureau can help you find this.

How the law works

There are no laws that list the exact rights and duties of parents. It is impossible to write down everything a parent should do for a child.

Instead, the law states that all married parents and unmarried mothers automatically have parental responsibility for their children. An unmarried father does not have automatic parental responsibility for his child. He can obtain parental responsibility by signing the birth register jointly with the mother, by agreement with her, by marrying her, or by being granted parental responsibility by the courts.

Parental responsibility This means having the responsibility and authority to care for the child's physical, moral, and emotional needs.

When a child or young person is taken into care, parental responsibility is given to the HSS trust, although parents do keep certain rights and responsibilities.

The law puts the interest of the child first. The powers that parents have to control their children are for the benefit of the child, not the parent. Those who deal with children in a legal setting, such as social workers, doctors and lawyers, must take careful note of what a child says, particularly when the child is able to understand all the issues involved. Parental responsibility ends when the child reaches 18. As a very experienced judge once said; "in law, parents begin with a right of control, but by the time the child is 18 they can do no more than advise."

Providing a home

Parents have a duty to look after and care for their children until they are 18. However, once someone reaches the age of 16 they can normally leave home without their parent's permission. The police and other authorities are unlikely to stop anyone leaving home, even against their parent's wishes, unless they are under 16, in some kind of danger, or are unable to look after themselves. See **home**, page 73.

Discipline

Parents have the right and duty to discipline their child - and this can include smacking. But corporal punishment must be "moderate and reasonable". If it is too harsh the parents risk prosecution or having their child's name put on the child protection register or the child being taken into care.

Education

Parents have a duty to make sure that their child has a suitable full-time education, between the ages of 4/5-16.
See **education**, page 24.

BABY-SITTING

Religion

Parents can decide the religion (if any) in which their child will be brought up. If they can't agree between themselves, they can go to court, where a judge will decide what is in the best interests of the child.

A court will listen to the views of the child concerned and these will be respected if the child clearly understands what is involved.

Medical treatment

In practice young people, aged 16 and over, can almost always agree to their own medical treatment without referring to their parents. Before treating a young person under 16, however, a doctor will normally try to obtain the parent's permission, unless it is an emergency or the young person is clearly able to understand what the treatment involves.

There is no law giving the minimum age for a baby-sitter, nor one stating how old a child must be before it can be left alone. Parents must take all the circumstances into account. For example, the age of the baby sitter, the availability of the parent(s) or the health of the children being looked after, count as relevant factors.

Parents have a legal duty to care for their children; some of that responsibility is temporarily passed on to a baby-sitter when the children are in their care. This means that parents must choose a baby-sitter who is able to look after their children properly. If a serious accident occurs while they are out, the parents may have to convince a court that they had done all that they could to make sure their child was being looked after properly. A baby-sitter under 16 will probably be thought too young to deal with an emergency.

adoption

Anyone who is under 18, and has never been married, can be adopted.

When a married couple wish to adopt a child, each partner must be at least 21. Single people may also apply to adopt a child if they have never been married or if they are separated from their marriage partner.

When children are adopted, they are treated in law almost as if they had been born to the couple or person who adopted them. Parents who adopt children are advised to be open about their child's birth family from the start.

At 18, people who have been adopted have the right to see a copy of their original birth records, and can get more information from the agency that arranged their adoption. An interview with a counsellor to prepare them for this is available.

Further help for adopted people and their birth relatives who wish to get in touch is available through the Register General for Northern Ireland and NORCAP. See life, page 6, and contacts.

living together

An increasing number of couples live together, sometimes with the thought of getting married later on, and sometimes not. Although this is a matter of personal choice, the law treats married and unmarried couples very differently.

Money and finance

A couple who live together without getting married are under no legal duty to look after one another, or to provide each other with financial support, unless it is something they have specifically agreed to do.

When children are involved, both parents, whether married or unmarried, have a legal responsibility to look after them and provide for them until they reach the age of 16, or up to 19 if they remain in full-time education.

If a married person dies without making a will, their partner is entitled to all or most of their possessions. But if they were not married, it can be very difficult for the partner to obtain any of the deceased's possessions.

Children

Parents who are married share parental responsibility for their children. This means that both can make decisions about their children's upbringing. Unmarried fathers have this right if the couple have signed a parental responsibility agreement, or if the father has made a successful application to court for parental responsibility or, since April 2002 if the father has jointly registered the birth of his child with the child's mother.

Home

A married couple have equal rights to occupy their home, whether they rent or own it. This continues even if their marriage fails, unless the court orders otherwise.

Unmarried couples may not have an automatic right to occupy the home, especially if the home is in just one person's name. In cases like this the non-owner may be able to apply to the court for a declaration of their ownership rights if they make mortgage payments or improvements to the structure of the property. Couples can avoid difficulties caused by this by using a solicitor to write a formal contract setting out what would happen to their house and contents etc should the relationship come to an end. However, these contracts may not be legally binding.

Breaking up

Unlike a married couple, people who live together can end their relationship anytime they choose, without having to go to court.

Getting married

Legally, no one can be forced to marry against their wishes, and each partner must be 16 or over and unmarried. A person who wants to marry, but is under 18, needs their parents' written consent. It's a criminal offence if a couple get married without this, but the marriage is still valid. However marriages involving someone aged 15 or under, or members of the same sex, are not recognised in law.

Almost anyone can be married in a Church of Ireland, Presbyterian or Roman Catholic church (unless they are divorced and their former partner is still alive) according to the traditions and rules of that church. Members of other faiths must, before the religious ceremony, obtain a civil certificate or licence from the senior registrar in the district where they live.

Under the *Marriage (NI) Order 2003*, couples can choose to marry in any registry office or in other places that have been approved (such as a hotel or stately home).

Being married to more than one person at the same time - called bigamy - is normally a crime. But the marriages may be recognised in Northern Ireland if they took place in a country that allows marriages of this kind, and if each partner was legally free to marry in that way.

Engagement

If someone breaks off their engagement there is usually not a duty to return the engagement ring. The ring is seen as a gift, and may be kept, unless it was originally agreed to return it if the marriage did not take place.

Civil partnerships

The *Civil Partnership Act (NI) Order 2005* allows same-sex couples, aged 16 and over, to register their partnership in a similar way to a civil marriage, and gives same-sex couples the same legal rights as people who marry. The law took effect from 21st December 2005 and means that same-sex couples have the same rights to property, benefits, inheritance and parental repsonsibility as those who are married.

The ceremony can take place in a registry office (or other licensed premises) – but not in a church or other religious building. There are indications, however, that some local authorities are reluctant to allow civil partnership ceremonies to take place on council property.

If either or both partners wish to end the partnership, a formal court process takes place, through which the partnership is dissolved.

VIOLENCE

A court can make orders to protect a victim of domestic violence and can order one partner to leave the home for the other's protection - even if they are married. It is important for anyone in this situation to get advice from a solicitor as soon as possible.

divorce

A couple who no longer wish to live together, can either end their marriage by divorce, or separate, keeping the marriage legally alive. A separation may simply mean living apart, or it can be made more formal through a court order called a judicial separation.

When one or both partners decide to divorce, an application is made to the county court or high court. It is made through a solicitor, (but not until at least two years after the date of marriage).

When the judge is satisfied that the appropriate arrangements have been made, that all the information is correct and that the marriage has broken down and cannot be saved, he or she will grant a decree nisi - the first stage in obtaining the divorce. Six weeks later, the person seeking the divorce can apply for a decree absolute. When this is granted, the marriage comes to an end.

Grounds for divorce

A person who applies for a divorce must prove to the court that their marriage has irretrievably broken down by showing that one of the following five things has happened....

1. the other partner has committed adultery, ie had sexual intercourse with someone of the opposite sex;

2. the other partner has behaved unreasonably. This covers many things, including violence, refusing to have children, gambling and alcoholism;

3. they have lived apart for two years, and they both want a divorce;

4. they have lived apart for five years and only one partner wants a divorce; or

5. one partner has deserted the other for at least two years immediately before the application.

Children

Parents going through a divorce are encouraged to reach an agreement between themselves over where their children will live and how often they will see each parent. But the judge will accept these arrangements only if satisfied that they are in the best interests of the child.

Parents who cannot agree over this are often advised not to go straight to court (expensive and stressful for all concerned), but to use independent mediators to help them sort out their problems. A court will, however, have to approve the final arrangements over children and money. It's usually felt to be in the children's interest to keep in touch with their family, so a judge will rarely stop a parent from seeing a child.

After the divorce, both parents usually always keep parental responsibility for their child, and both should consult each other over decisions that affect their child's life, such as education, medical treatment, and religious upbringing.

Step-parents

Step-parents do not automatically have parental responsibility for their stepchildren, but the courts can require them to support a step-child. With their new partner, the step-parent may help with day-to-day things affecting the child, but major decisions should be taken by the child's birth mother and father - or only the mother, if they were not married (unless the father has parental responsibility). To change this, a step-parent may apply for parental responsibility order or, together with the birthparent, to adopt the child. See **contacts** for organisations able to give more information about this.

Grandparents

When a marriage ends, it may mean that a child is prevented from seeing other family members, such as grandparents, adding to the child's loss. In some situations, grandparents can apply to a court for permission to carry on seeing the child or to have the child stay with them.

Family disputes

Sometimes parents become involved in legal disputes which directly affect their children - especially if they are getting divorced and cannot agree who the children should live with. Children's views are usually reflected through a social worker or court welfare officer. See **contacts** for specialist advice.

home

young citizen's **passport**

INDIVIDUALS
ENGAGING IN
SOCIETY

Citizenship Foundation

a place of your own

Where do I look?

Advertisements for accommodation are found in local newspapers, supermarkets and the student union, if you are at college. The Northern Ireland Housing Executive can tell you whether you are likely to qualify for public housing, and can also give you details of local housing associations.

You can also try estate agents and accommodation agencies. These agencies are not allowed, by law, to charge you for information about housing or lists of vacancies. Don't agree to pay them a fee. Normally they are paid for their services by the landlord. If you are asked for money and have any doubts, check first with the local Citizens Advice Bureau, Housing Rights Service or the Housing Executive, see **contacts**. Don't be rushed. It's a good idea to get someone to look at the place with you.

You can't buy or rent a house or get a mortgage if you are under 18.

What's the rent? What does it include - rates, electricity etc? How often is it paid, and who is it paid to? Is any rent payable in advance? Rent paid in advance will be lost if you leave without giving the right amount of notice.

Your rent will usually be fixed at whatever rate you agree with your landlord. A small group of older rented houses have their rents fixed by government. To check if this applies to you, contact the Housing Executive or the Housing Rights Service.

Do I pay a deposit? This is an amount (often equal to a month's rent) paid to the landlord, or the agent, at the start of the tenancy. Always ask for a receipt when you hand over your deposit.

If you cause damage or leave bills

HOUSING BENEFIT

If you are on a training programme, Income Support or a low wage, you may qualify for Housing Benefit from the Housing Executive. The Housing Executive District Office or Citizens Advice Bureau can help you work out what you're entitled to. Housing Benefit is not available to full-time students, unless they have children or have a disability.

If you're out of work and on Housing Benefit, you may find that you lose your Housing Benefit when you start working – which could make it difficult to keep on your flat or house.

Housing Benefit for most single people under 25 will not be more than the average rent of a single room in the area.

use the law with care **try talking first**

by this figure and decide whether it seems reasonable. If you rent your home from a private landlord or a housing association and pay a variable service charge as well as rent, you have the right to ask the landlord exactly how the service charge is calculated.

Do I need references? If so, choose people who have known you for a reasonable length of time, but preferably not a close relative. It is important to ask the person concerned first.

How safe? Check the fire escape, plumbing, electrical fittings, and heating appliances. Landlords must, by law, have all gas appliances checked each year and must get a certificate of safety that you are entitled to see.

or rent unpaid, the landlord can take what you owe from your deposit. Try to agree any deductions with the landlord before you leave, otherwise you may find you've lost more of your deposit than you should.

Is there a service charge? This is money paid to look after the building and clean those parts that are shared, such as the stairs and corridors in a block of flats. Check what is covered

---

Discrimination

In general, a landlord must not discriminate against a would-be tenant on grounds of religion, race or sex. Likewise someone who sells or lets property should not discriminate against a potential buyer on the grounds of religion, race, sex or disability.

Leaving home

Young people under 18 are still, in law, in the "custody and care" of their parents, which means that, strictly speaking, they need their parent's permission to leave home. But, in reality, courts are unlikely to order anyone aged 16 or 17 to return home who leaves home against their parents' wishes, unless they appear to

be in some kind of danger or unable to look after themselves. See also **family**, page 64.

If you are 16 or 17 and homeless, or feel that you can no longer live at home because you are being hurt, or because life at home is so bad, you can get help from social services. Under the *Children Order (NI) 1995*, Health Trusts have the power to provide accommodation for 16 and 17 year olds whose welfare would be endangered if accommodation were not provided. Income Support is not available to all 16 or 17 year olds. Therefore, if you can, get advice from a Housing Executive District Office or Citizens Advice Bureau before you do anything.

In care If you are leaving care, your local social services have a legal duty to provide help and advice.

When you rent a flat or house, you normally sign an agreement with the landlord or their agent. This is known in law as a tenancy agreement, sometimes called a lease.

It should contain all the conditions agreed between you and the landlord, along with a list (called an inventory) of the furniture and other equipment that comes with the property. Make sure everything is included, and make a note of anything that's damaged when you take up the property.

All private landlords in Northern Ireland have a legal obligation to provide their tenants with a rent book free of charge. The rent book must include information such as the rent and any other

charges payable, the landlord and any agent's name, etc.

Read all documents carefully. Don't be afraid to seek advice from the Citizens Advice Bureau, Housing Executive District Office, or a solicitor if parts are not clear, or if they contain conditions which you didn't expect. Don't sign until you fully understand the agreement and are prepared to accept what it says.

Normally you and the landlord will sign two copies of the tenancy agreement and keep a copy of each. Look after this. If there's any kind of problem while you're in the property, you'll need it to check your rights and duties.

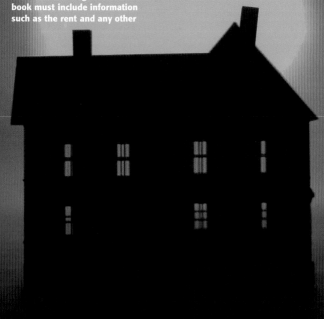

use the law with care try talking first

Lodging and hostels

You do not have the same rights if you are in lodgings or if your landlord lives with you in the same house and shares the basic services with you. Your landlady or landlord only needs to give you "reasonable notice" (this can be seven days), and does not need to apply to a court to have you evicted.

If you are in hostel accommodation, the hostel provider will not generally need a court order to evict you. They can give you notice at any time, as long as they keep to the terms of the tenancy agreement.

Northern Ireland Housing Executive tenants

You have certain rights as a Housing Executive tenant, which include staying in your house for as long as you want (assuming you pay your rent and do what your tenancy agreement says), taking in lodgers, and being consulted about the running of the estate. The Housing Executive may take action against tenants who cause a nuisance to others on the estate. In serious cases this may lead to tenants losing their homes, see page 20.

Repairs and maintenance

Who is responsible?

Unless your tenancy agreement says otherwise, your landlord is responsible for looking after the structure of the building, including outside fittings (such as gutters) and essential services (heating appliances - not cookers - sinks, baths and toilets and the water, gas and electricity supplies). Responsibility for other repairs depends on what is said in the tenancy agreement. Tenants are normally responsible for repairs for damage that they cause, but not for fair "wear and tear".

Getting them done

Tell the landlord when the repairs need doing - and keep paying the rent. If the landlord does nothing and the problem concerns serious questions of health and safety, you can get in touch with the Housing Executive District Office or the local environmental health department. They have the powers to get something done, and can make the landlord carry out the necessary work. Their number is in the phone book under the name of your District Council.

If the problem is not serious, or the District Council won't take action, check again that responsibility for the work lies with your landlord. If it does, write to the landlord explaining you intend to undertake the work yourself and send at least three estimates of the cost. Give your landlord at least two weeks to consider these. If, at the end of this period, there is still no sign that the repairs will be carried out, you may go ahead with them yourself, taking the cost from your rent. Keep detailed records of everything you've done and a copy of every letter you write and receive. If you are in any doubt, at any stage, seek advice.

> Dear Landlord
> As I told you by (phone/letter) on (date), the water heater at (the address) is broken, and it is your responsibility to put this right under our tenancy agreement. Since this has not been done, I have got (three) estimates for repairs from (names and addresses of firms), which I enclose. Unless I hear from you by (date) that you will do these repairs straightaway, I will have no option but to ask (name your choice) to do the repair. I shall then deduct their bill from future rental payments
> Yours sincerely,

Eviction

Generally speaking, you cannot be made to leave the house or flat that you are renting, unless the landlord has given you notice in the correct way and obtained a possession order from a court. In most cases, it is a criminal offence for anyone to evict you without a court order, or to try to force you out with threats. Court orders are generally not necessary, however, if you live in lodgings or your landlord lives on the premises. But your landlord still can't use violence to force you to leave. This is an offence under the *Rent (NI) Order 1978*.

If you're threatened with eviction, get advice straightaway from a solicitor or your Housing Executive District Office or Citizens Advice Bureau. Make sure you keep on paying the rent. Failure to pay will make it easier for the landlord to require you to leave.

Harrassment If your landlord stops short of physical violence, but still behaves in a way designed to make you leave - like changing the locks, shouting abuse or playing loud music - they will be breaking the *Rent (NI) Order 1978*. Again your Housing Executive District Office or Citizens Advice Bureau can help. If physical violence is used or threatened, call the police.

▮ BRIEF CASE: Laurie

A few weeks after signing a six-month tenancy agreement for a bed-sit, Laurie was told to leave. His landlord had decided to sell the house and knew he would get more money for it with Laurie out of his room. The lock on Laurie's door was taken off, and the landlord threatened to tip his possessions into a black plastic bag. Without a job, Laurie spent more than two months sleeping in his car. With legal advice, and using legal aid, he took his case to court. The judge decided Laurie had been illegally evicted and ordered the landlord to pay him £36,500 in compensation - the extra amount of money the landlord made by selling his house without a tenant.

Insurance If you are living in rented accommodation, insurance for the building is normally arranged by the owner, but it's worth checking exactly what this covers. Building insurance will not cover the cost of replacing your things if they are damaged or stolen. You can arrange to insure your belongings through an insurance company or a broker, see **money**, pages 58-59.

If you have anything valuable, like a camera, stereo or jewellery, you will need to list it separately on the insurance and find out exactly how much it costs to replace. The same applies to something like a bike that may be stolen or lost outside the home.

Some policies will give you the full replacement cost; others take into account wear and tear, and pay you less. If you are under insured it means that your belongings are insured for less than their real value. If the insurance company discovers this when you make a claim, the amount they pay out is likely to be reduced.

Noisy neighbours The best way to tackle a problem of noise, or any other nuisance, is to talk to the person concerned, if possible, before the situation gets out of hand. Sometimes this is easier and more effective if several people complain together. If this doesn't work, write a simple letter (keep a copy), and allow a reasonable time for your neighbour to respond.

If that fails, get in touch with your district council environmental health department. They have powers to investigate and deal with the matter. See also **leisure**, page 86.

homelessness

Housing Executive help If you are homeless, the Housing Executive should be able to help. It has a legal duty to give you advice and help towards finding somewhere to live, but this is not the same as offering you somewhere to stay. The Housing Executive has to house you only if you are 16 or over and

- **homeless; and**
- **in priority need; and**
- **have a connection with the local area; and**
- **have not made yourself intentionally homeless.**

You should qualify as a priority need if

- **you're pregnant; or**
- **you have a child who depends on you; or**
- **you've had to leave your last home because someone was violent towards you; or**
- **you've lost your home through something like a fire or flood; or**
- **your age, health problems or disability makes you vulnerable and unable to cope with being homeless; or**
- **you are under 21 and at risk of sexual exploitation.**

Sleeping rough This is dangerous, and places the person at risk of being assaulted. Without an address, it is harder to get a job and even benefit. Someone found sleeping rough or begging more than once may be fined.

SQUATTING

A squatter is someone who enters and occupies land, or any part of a building, without the owner's permission. Squatting is not a crime, but squatters may commit an offence if they cause damage when getting into the property or to the contents, or by using gas or electricity without first making the proper arrangements.

If squatters leave a place empty, the owner can break in and take possession, but may commit an offence if force is used while the squatters are still inside. An owner or tenant who intends to move in immediately and use the property as a place of residence, may use reasonable force in getting a squatter to leave, but normally requires a written statement or certificate showing that the property is needed as a home. In this situation a squatter commits an offence in refusing to leave.

Squatters can also be evicted from a property through the issue of a possession order by a court. There are a number of different types of order but, in some circumstances, squatters may have only 24 hours to leave and may not return to the property within the next twelve months.

Advice is available for anyone considering squatting, see **contacts**.

leisure

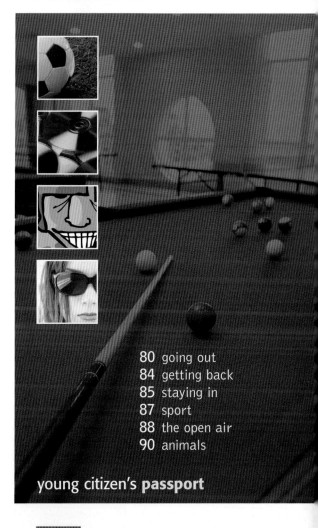

young citizen's **passport**

INDIVIDUALS ENGAGING IN SOCIETY

Citizenship Foundation

going out

It may be for fun, but you don't leave your legal rights at home when you go out for the night. If you spend an evening at a match or concert looking at nothing more than a roof support or girder, then you have a right to complain and ask for a refund. It's no excuse for the management to say that you should have arrived earlier for a better seat. Under the law of contract they should have warned you that the view was restricted before selling you the tickets.

There is no simple law setting out people's rights in the event of a change to the advertised programme or the cancellation of a performance. Your legal position will depend on such things as advance publicity, information given when the ticket was sold and the circumstances that forced a change of plan.

Although disgruntled spectators have been successful in taking promoters to court, legal action is not recommended for disappointment over a cancelled event. Some promoters will try to retain goodwill by offering tickets for another performance, or refunds. If they don't, it's worth explaining why you think their action is unreasonable - a key word in cases of this kind.

Pubs and off-licences

The licensing laws controlling the sale of drinks were introduced at the beginning of the 20th century, and it's only in the last few years that they have begun to change.

Providing they sell soft drinks and food, pubs can now apply for a children's certificate allowing children under 18, accompanied by an adult, into a bar. The children, however, have to leave by 9pm.

Only when you're 18 can you buy alcohol or drink alcohol in a bar or be present in a bar without an adult. Drinks with 0.5 per cent or less of alcohol, such as some canned shandy and low alcohol beers, are treated as non-alcoholic.

If you are found on unlicensed premises where alcohol is being served, whether or not you are drinking, it is likely that you are guilty of an offence.

It is an offence to sell alcohol to anyone under 18 - unless it can be shown that the landlord did their best to check the person was 18 or over. It's also an offence for you to buy, or try to buy, alcohol if you are under 18, or to buy or try to buy it for someone under 18. The landlord may be fined or serve a six month jail sentence, and licensees stand to lose their licence after more than one conviction.

The measures of alcohol that you can be sold are legally controlled. A reasonable head forms part of a pint of beer. The prices of drinks and food should be displayed by law, and should be clearly visible from where the drinks are served.

REFUSING TO SERVE

Pubs and off-licences can refuse to serve anyone with drink who looks as if they've had enough already, otherwise they can be charged with 'permitting drunkenness' and fined. Licensees have the right to ban or refuse to serve anyone they choose - unless it is because of their sex, religion, ethnic group or disability.

use the law with care **try talking first**

Not in public If a young person under 18 is in a public place (e.g. the street), or a place they have entered illegally, and have been drinking, or are about to drink, the police or another accredited person can, under the *Confiscation of Alcohol (Young Persons) Act 1997*, require them to stop drinking and can take away the alcohol. Refusal may lead to arrest or a fine of up to £500.

They can also take alcohol from someone over 18 who is in a public place, if they believe it will be passed to under-age drinkers.

The police can ask for the name and address of anyone from whom they have taken alcohol in these circumstances, and it is an offence to refuse to give these details or to give a false name and address.

All 26 district councils have by-laws that make it illegal to drink alcohol in designated areas and that give the police the power to take the names and addresses of offenders. This information may be passed to the local council which is responsible for prosecution.

Proof of age If you have trouble proving you are over 18, you can apply for a proof of age card, carrying your name, photograph, date of birth and signature. Cards are available from Citizencard or the Portman Group - an organisation sponsored by the UK's major drinks companies - and a card costs £5. Application forms are available online or from pubs, off-licences and supermarkets, see **contacts**.

Eating out

Quality Whether you're in an expensive restaurant or an ordinary takeaway you have the right to reject any food of a quality below the standard that you are reasonably entitled to expect. What is 'reasonable' depends on such things as the price charged, what the menu says, and basic standards. The laws applying to faulty goods or services also apply. See also **money**, pages 48-51.

Complaints It's advisable to complain as soon as you know there's a problem and before eating food you believe is unsatisfactory. The more you are paying the higher the standard you're entitled to expect.

If the quality of your meal is poor or the service is bad, you are entitled to make a reasonable deduction from the bill, but don't leave without paying. Explain to the manager why you are not satisfied, and leave your name and address. It is then up to the restaurant to take this up with you later on if they wish.

Price All restaurants, pubs and cafés must, by law, clearly display the price of food and drink where it is served, so you can read it before you order or sit down at a table.

Service charge A service charge may sometimes be added to the bill in a restaurant. It is usually around ten per cent. If it was made clear before you ordered that service will be included, then you have got to pay it. If the service was unsatisfactory, see the manager to ask for a discount. If there is no service charge included, it is up to you whether to leave a tip.

Safety Under the *Food Safety (NI) Order 1991*, it is an offence for a restaurant to serve food that is unfit for human consumption. If you are concerned about the hygiene in a place where you have eaten, you can contact your district council environmental health department, which has the power to investigate.

Fireworks

Indoor fireworks and sparklers are legal, but in 2002 new regulations were introduced to deal with outdoor fireworks because they were being used in riots. In Northern Ireland, you must have a have a licence for even the smallest private display. It is an offence if you are found with outdoor fireworks and do not have a licence and may be fined up to £5,000. You can apply to the Northern Ireland Office for a licence.

use the law with care **try talking first**

GAMBLING

Anyone under 18 is forbidden from going into a betting shop, private club, or into an amusement arcade with gaming machines offering all cash prizes of £10 or more.

Lottery tickets or scratch cards should not be sold to anyone under 16 and winnings cannot be collected by someone below this age.

If you're under 18, you are only allowed into a licensed bingo club if you don't take part.

Gambling contracts cannot be enforced in law. If the loser fails to pay, he or she cannot be taken to court. Therefore, if you bet, it's wise to use a reputable bookie.

Nightclubs

Nightclubs must have special licences for entertainment and the sale of alcohol. Like pubs, it's illegal to sell alcohol to someone under 18, and owners are within their rights to choose who they will or will not allow in, as long as they do not break the anti-discrimination laws. Clubs who charge lower entry fees for women than men are breaking the law.

The door

Bouncers have no special legal powers. The same laws apply to them as everyone else, which means that they can only use a reasonable amount of force to throw someone out. In certain circumstances this means no force at all - and a bouncer who uses too much force without good reason commits an offence.

getting back

Taxis in Northern Ireland

Taxis in Northern Ireland are under licensing control, which is the responsibilty of the Department of the Environment. The vehicles must be checked annually and drivers must meet requirements relating to health and character. But unlike London and Dublin drivers, they do not have to pass a 'knowledge' test to get their licence.

Public hire taxis can be flagged down, as well as hired, from a taxi rank. From a rank a taxi driver cannot unreasonably refuse to take a fare.

It is a criminal offence for a driver of a cab to lengthen the journey in time or distance without cause. Fares are regulated by law for Belfast public hire taxis operating within a five mile radius of the city centre.

Under the *Disability Discrimination Act 1995*, Belfast Public hire taxis have to be fully accessible to disabled travellers. Public hire taxi drivers are also required to help disabled people in and out of taxis and to help with their luggage - although drivers can claim exemption from this if they have a back injury that prevents them from lifting heavy objects.

Private hire taxis

Private hire taxis may be booked in advance or in person at a taxi depot. Even if there's a meter, it's a good idea to get an estimate of the fare before you set off or agree the fare in advance. Private hire taxis are generally unaffected by the *Disability Discrimination Act*.

Unlicensed taxis

Unlike black cabs or licensed taxis, these vehicles will not have been specially examined and may not even have a current MOT. They will not be insured to carry fare-paying passengers, so passengers have little protection if anything goes wrong. All licensed taxis are required to display distinctive licence plates.

No entry

The driver of a licensed taxi or hire car who, without good reason, refuses to take a passenger (including a disabled person) may be prosecuted and fined. Anyone who feels that they are a victim of this, and wishes to do something about it, should make a note of the plate or registration number of the taxi or hire vehicle and report it to their DVLNI, who will investigate the case and then prosecute the driver if they feel there is sufficient evidence.

use the law with care try talking first

Parties

Drink and drugs

Although you can't buy alcohol from an off-licence until you're 18, anyone over 14 can drink alcohol on private premises. It is an offence to give alcohol to a child under 14, unless for medical purposes.

An offence is committed, under the *Misuse of Drugs Act 1971*, if you knowingly allow anyone into your flat or house to supply an illegal drug to someone else, or allow the smoking of cannabis. Even if you are not taking the drug yourself, you can still be charged, as it is your place they are using. The penalty for someone allowing their flat or house to be used for drug-taking is up to 14 years in prison for a Class A or B drug, or five years for a Class C drug. For more on the law and drugs, see **life** pages 10-13.

Safety

You invite some friends around for the evening and one of them falls down the stairs. If the cause of the accident was the state of the carpet rather than too much beer, you or your parents could be liable for their injuries. This doesn't mean wrapping every sharp corner in cotton wool, but something like a loose piece of stair carpet definitely should be fixed, since it is reasonable for visitors to expect to walk down the stairs safely. You're not expected to guard against the unforeseeable. If someone slides down the banisters and breaks a leg, then that's their problem.

Insurance

If someone is injured in your home you could be required to pay them compensation - although this can be paid through an insurance policy, if you have one. Most householders' insurance policies cover owners for injuries to other people called "third parties" caused by the state of the buildings or its fittings. If you're in rented accommodation, your landlord could be liable - and again it is his or her insurance company that would pay damages. If you face this problem you can check with a solicitor or Citizens Advice Bureau.

Gatecrashing

Gatecrashing is trespass. The law says that you can use reasonable force to get gatecrashers to leave, but don't start waving a broken bottle around. This is unreasonable and will leave you in more trouble than them.

staying in

Noise If there is a noisy party and the police are called, they can ask people to be quiet, but there's not much else they can do unless they fear there's going to be a breach of the peace - that is some kind of disorder. Then arrests will almost certainly be made.

However, if you are being disturbed by noise from a neighbour between 11pm and 7am, you can ring the district council environmental health department, which must investigate your complaint as soon as possible. Under the *Noise Act 1996*, they have the power to send an officer to the house to measure the noise and decide whether it is excessive. If it is, the person believed to be responsible will be given a warning notice, requiring the noise to be switched off or turned down within ten minutes. An offence is committed if the noise continues, the officer can decide to prosecute or issue an on-the-spot fine of £100. If an on-the-spot fine is paid within 14 days no further legal action can be taken for the offence; if it is not paid, a court can impose a higher fine.

If the warning notice is ignored, the officer can also obtain a warrant (often very quickly) to go into the building and remove the sound equipment that is being used.

For other problems with noisy neighbours, see **home**, page 77.

TV, video, music, and the Internet You need a TV licence if you use a TV or any other equipment to receive or record TV programmes (such as DVD or VCR, a set-top box or a PC with a video card). Failure to have a valid licence can result in a court appearance and a fine of up to £1,000. One licence covers all the equipment in a single home. If rooms are rented separately, a license must be obtained for the TV equipment in each room. Students living away from home are generally not covered by their parents' licence, unless they are using a small pocket-sized TV, powered by internal batteries. Students who live in a hall of residence and have a TV in their room need their own TV licence.

Taping and recording You can tape or record a TV or radio programme for your own use, but only to listen to at a more convenient time. Strictly speaking, it's against the law to record a programme just because you find it particularly enjoyable or to keep it as part of a collection. Copying a CD, tape or computer game belonging to someone else is also illegal.

The Internet All music and recordings of music are copyrighted (that is owned by someone) - for at least 50 years from the date on which they were created.

Downloading music files (whether for personal use or for profit) from the Net is a

■ BRIEF CASE

The EasyInternetCafé burned CDs of internet downloads (including MP3 music) on behalf of their customers and for profit. Some of the downloads were Sony's copyright and they successfully sued the Café to stop it being done.

breach of copyright and is illegal, unless it is done with permission from the record label. The key point in law is that the person responsible has obtained for free something that they would normally have to buy.

Over the past year, the British record industry has started legal action against a number of people they have discovered either down- or uploading music. Lists of legal digital music services are available from the industry's website, www.bpi.co.uk.

sport

Risks and the duty of care

Anyone who plays sport must expect to suffer the sorts of injuries normal to the game concerned. But intentional or reckless damage to someone else is another matter, and the player responsible, referee or organisers can be sued for damages and prosecuted for a criminal offence. Organisers of sporting events also have a duty to see that visitors, spectators and passers-by are reasonably safe.

■ BRIEF CASE: Football

A Stockport County player was awarded £250,000 after his career was ended through injuries suffered in a match against Swansea City. The court decided that he was brought down by a tackle aimed at the legs, rather than the ball, which did not reflect the reasonable care that players should show towards one another.

the open air

Walking

All land in Northern Ireland is owned by someone - private landowners, a local authority, government body, or the Crown.

You will not usually end up in court by stepping on to a piece of land marked "trespassers will be prosecuted". Trespass is not a crime (unless you also cause damage) - it's a civil offence. A landowner can require the trespasser to leave, but in doing so may use only a reasonable amount of force. If the trespasser refuses to go, the landowner should call the police.

Footpaths

If a route across a piece of land has been used for 20 years or more without interruption, that route may become a right of way. It is very unlikely that a footpath will be lost through disuse.

Strictly speaking, footpaths are for walkers only. It can be a criminal offence to drive a motorbike or car on a path. Footpaths are usually shown on Ordnance Survey Discoverer maps - but if you need to check on a path, you can ask to look at the maps in the district council offices.

Under the *Access to the Countryside (NI) Order 1983*, a landowner may be able to plough or plant any crop over a public footpath, the landowner must reinstate the surface of a path within 14 days. It is an offence to put up a misleading sign, such as "private" that discourages people from using a public right of way. If you come across a problem of this kind and want something done, contact the district council.

The district council has a duty to make sure that public rights of way are kept open and free from obstruction. It's the district council's responsibility to maintain footpaths so that people can walk along them, and the job of the landowner to look after stiles and gates along the path or footpath.

The *Access to the Countryside (NI) Order 1983* enables the public to be given access to land designated as open country. Landowners can impose restrictions on how the land is accessed or used. You can check with the district council to see which land is open, see **contacts**.

BULLS

Checking your legal rights here needs some farming knowledge and the ability to tell one breed of bull from another without getting too close. All dairy bulls (breeds like Friesian, Guernsey and Jersey) are banned from fields crossed by public paths. Other types of bull are allowed only if they are in with cows or heifers, which apparently makes them much less aggressive.

use the law with care **try talking first**

Rivers, canals and the sea

There is a public right to use a canoe or boat only on the tidal section of a river. Beyond this point you need permission from the owner of the riverbank to use the river.

Waterways Ireland is responsible for the Erne system and the Lower Bann. There are no licence fees as such, although you may have to pay charges for launching, using locks and berthing. You can get information about canoeing from the Canoe Association of Northern Ireland.

Anyone is free to use a boat or to water-ski or jet-ski on the sea although, in harbours, ferries and other shipping have a right of way.

Fishing

You can fish in the sea and in tidal waters at any time, unless there are local by-laws forbidding it. There are two licensing authorities: the Fisheries Conservancy Board for Northern Ireland (www.fcbni.com) issues licences for most areas except for the Carlingford and Foyle catchments where they are issued by the Loughs Agency (www.loughs-agency.org). In the FCB area anyone over 12 years of age needs a rod licence to fish in rivers and loughs. In the Lough's Agency area everyone needs a licence with a reduction for juveniles under the age of 18. You will also need a permit from the fishery owner.

Pollution

The Environment and Heritage Agency asks members of the public to report any urgent environmental incident relating to water pollution by ringing the Environment and Heritage Agency Water Pollution Hotline 0800 80 70 60. Less urgent incidents may be reported by mail at the address Emergency-Pollution@doeni.gov.uk

Beaches

Land between the low and high tide lines is the property of the Crown - but there is almost never a problem in walking along a beach. However, there is no right to get onto a beach over private land, unless there is a public right of way.

◼ BRIEF CASE: Katrina

Katrina noticed that the water in Ackhurst Brook near Wigan, where she lived, was an unusual colour - particularly around the discharge pipe used by a local factory. She rang the Environment Agency (in Northern Ireland this would be the Environment and Heritage Service) who sent an officer to investigate. The officer reported that the water was discoloured and smelt foul and contained pieces of food that looked like shells from baked beans - which is just what they were. The company admitted polluting the river and was fined £5,000.

animals

Wildlife

The *Wildlife (NI) Order 1985* protects a wide range of wild animals, birds and plants and covers killing, injuring, taking or possessing and disturbing their place of shelter or protection. Information on endangered species and habitats in Northern Ireland is available on the Environment and Heritage Service website at www.ehsni.gov.uk.

Pets

Under the *Welfare of Animals (NI) Act 1972*, a pet owner has a legal responsibility to care for the animal and make sure it does not suffer unnecessarily. It is also an offence to be cruel to the animal or to abandon it if it is likely to cause the animal unnecessary suffering.

Pet owners are also responsible for any damage their animal causes if they knew (or should have known) it was likely to cause such damage, or if their animal is defined as dangerous.

Under a proposed new law for Northern Ireland (*Dangerous Wild Animal (NI) Order 2004*, a licence will be needed by anyone who wants to keep a wild and dangerous animal. They will to have show that they can keep the animal securely and that they can look after it properly.

Dogs

Under the *Dogs (NI) Order 1983*, a person keeping a dog must have a licence. Anyone owning a dog must make sure that it wears a collar with the name and address of its owner when it is in a public place. If a dog fouls a footpath, the person in charge of the dog commits an offence if he or she fails to clear up the mess.

It is an offence under the *Dangerous Dogs (NI) Order 1991*, to allow a dog to be dangerously out of control in a public place. The owner, or person in charge, of the dog can be fined or imprisoned for up to six months. The court can also order the dog to be destroyed, and can disqualify the owner from keeping a dog in the future. A farmer is allowed to shoot a dog that is not under anyone's control and is worrying livestock on their land.

Under the *Guard Dogs Control Order (NI) 1985*, guard dogs should be under the control of a handler or else tied up and prevented from roaming freely. A warning notice should also be displayed.

▨ BRIEF CASE: Lisa

When Lisa had to go away unexpectedly, she said that she asked a friend to feed and water her pet rat, Ziggy. After Lisa had been gone for six days, one of Lisa's neighbours told the RSPCA that the animal was in need of care. They found the rat with just a scrap of cheese and no water. It was dehydrated, trembling, and close to death. Lisa, who was unemployed, was fined £80 and told to pay £50 towards the cost of the case.

brief case

CONTACTS see pages 134-143 for organisations able to give help & advice

travel
and transport

young citizen's passport

INDIVIDUALS ENGAGING IN SOCIETY

Citizenship Foundation

Package holidays

When you book a holiday, you are making a contract with the tour organiser - that is the company responsible for arranging the package. This is usually the tour operator, but it can also be the travel agent, particularly if you have asked for extra arrangements to be made, not included in the brochure.

Although holiday brochures are designed to show the hotel or resort at its best, the *Package Travel, Package Holidays and Package Tours Regulations 1992* state that they must be accurate and not misleading. If the room or the swimming pool that you were promised is not available, you may be able to claim compensation because of the failure of the company arranging the holiday to keep its side of the contract. It is an offence, under the *Trade Descriptions Act 1968*, for a firm to make a statement that it knows to be false about the goods or services it provides. Prosecutions for this are usually made by local trading standards officers.

It's important to inform the travel agent or tour operator of any special needs at the time you make the booking.

Before you sign or hand over any money, read the small print and to check what it says about changes to your schedule. Under certain circumstances, travel organisers can alter flight times or accommodation arrangements provided they make this clear in the brochure or contract. If you pay all or part of the cost of the holiday by credit card, you may be entitled to claim a full or partial refund from the credit card company if the firm organising the holiday fails to keep its side of the contract. For more information on paying by credit card, see **money** page 54.

TRAVEL AND MEDICAL INSURANCE

Travel insurance will protect you from losses while you're away and even illness before you go.

Take the policy with you on holiday, so that if anything goes wrong you can make sure you keep to the terms of the agreement.

BEFORE YOU GO

- **Check whether you need to have any vaccinations, and think about getting medical insurance, see below.**

- **If you are travelling in the European Union, apply for a European Health Insurance Card (EHIC) – allowing free or reduced medical costs – and take it with you on holiday. If you have to see a doctor, or go to hospital, and don't have an EHIC, you may have to pay for your medical expenses.**

An application form is available from a post office or at www.dh.gov.uk/travellers You can also apply by phone by calling 0845 606 2030.

- **Check your passport is up to date and whether you need a visa for the country you are visiting.**

If you need to know more about travel requirements or conditions, ring the embassy of the country concerned.

use the law with care try talking first

If you go abroad, book through a travel company registered with ABTA, IATA or ATOL. If the travel firm belongs to one of these organisations, you'll find their symbol in the brochure. They will cover the cost of getting you home, or compensate you for your losses if the company you've booked with goes bust while you're away, or before you've left.

UK Passports Everyone who travels abroad, including young children, must have their own passport. However, children already included on someone else's passport before October 1998 can continue to travel abroad with the passport holder until either the child reaches 16, the passport expires or is submitted for amendment.

Irish Passports Children may be included on a parent's passport and, as long as they are travelling with the parent, can travel to most countries until they are 16. Children may also have their own passport and may apply for a three or ten year version.

If something goes wrong If there is a problem with the holiday that the travel company has provided, tell them or their representative as soon as possible. If you're still not satisfied, make a note of the facts (photographic evidence may be helpful), and then contact the travel firm as soon as you get home.

If you're not satisfied with their reply, write to the managing director of the travel firm. If the company belongs to ABTA, you can have your claim decided by an independent person called an arbitrator. If this is not possible, get advice from the Citizens Advice Bureau and, if necessary, a solicitor. Going to court is a last resort.

If your luggage doesn't arrive, report the loss immediately. Try to obtain a copy of any reports that you complete. Under international law, the airline is responsible for lost or damaged luggage, but compensation is paid by weight not value, and the airline is not responsible for fragile items. It may be better to claim through your holiday insurance.

If you lose all your cash and your cards, you can go to a bank and arrange for money to be transferred from home. There will probably be a charge, but it should arrive within 24 hours.

If you lose anything valuable, tell the police and get a note from them confirming that you have done this. Contact the travel company if you lose your ticket home, and immediately report the loss of traveller's cheques or credit cards to the company offices. They often let you reverse the charges for the call. It is very important to report losses to your insurance company within the time limit stated in the policy.

If your Irish or British passport is lost or stolen, contact the Irish or British Consulate who have an office in most big cities and should be able to give you help or advice.

In trouble Travellers overseas are automatically subject to the laws of the country they are visiting.

If you're arrested, insist on the British Consulate being informed. The Consulate will explain the local procedures, including access to a lawyer and the availability of legal aid. A European Union (EU) national can go to any EU Consulate. See **the european union** page 128.

Taking a car or motorcycle

You'll normally need to get a Green Card from your insurance company, which extends your motor insurance to countries other than the UK.

If your car is insured in Northern Ireland you will probably not need a Green Card to travel to the Republic of Ireland unless you are travelling for business.

It is also worth checking with a motoring organisation such as the AA, RAC and Green Flag, whether you need an International Driving Permit, who can issue one too.

If you're driving to Spain, you should also take out a Bail Bond (fianza). Under Spanish law, the car and driver can be detained after an accident, but can be released on production of a Bail Bond. The Bond will also help cover the cost of any legal action or fine. Contact your motor insurance company for both the Green Card and Bail Bond.

If you have an accident, tell the police and ask for a record or receipt. It will help with your insurance claim when you get home. For the same reason, it's also a good idea to take notes and photographs of the incident, including pictures of the number plates of the vehicles involved.

Don't sign anything in a language that you don't understand. If you're put under pressure, write "I don't understand" immediately above your signature.

Coming home

If you are returning from a country within the EU, you do not have to pay customs charges on any goods you bought in that country, but nor can you obtain any duty-free concessions. However, there is generally no limit on the amount you can bring in – as long as the goods are for a gift or your own use.

Limits are, however, placed on alcohol and tobacco and anyone who exceeds these must convince the customs that the goods are not going to be sold on. No one under 17 is entitled to a tobacco or alcohol allowance.

Customs officials can check your baggage for prohibited goods or to see if you need to pay any tax or duty if you have been to a country outside the EU. Details of the powers and duties of customs officers are given in the Traveller's Charter, available from libraries and the Customs website: www.hmce.gov.uk/public/travel

Buses and trains

Translink tickets

On Translink services within Northern Ireland, young people are entitled to a 50 per cent discount until the 30 June following their sixteenth birthday. Between the ages of 16 and 21 reductions are only available on train season tickets. You can apply for a proof of age card at main stations. If you are able to prove that you are unemployed or are on the Gateway period of the New Deal, you may be able to get fares at a reduced rate.

The Translink Student Discount Cards are available to fulltime students and school pupils over 12. They may be obtained from main train and bus stations and cost £7. They give up to 33 per cent reductions on many Translink fares including cross border fares and some Bus Éireann services.

use the law with care try talking first

Iarnród Éireann (Irish Rail) and Dublin Bus offer two types of Student TravelCard: a City card (€10) for commuter services and a National card (€15). If you are studying in the Republic of Ireland, you may wish to buy one of these. They are available from main stations.

- **An Inter-Rail Pass gives you at least 16 days' rail travel in Continental Europe from £159, with discounts available on Eurostar and many cross Channel ferries. You must be under 26, be a citizen of or have lived in Europe for at least six months and have a passport. Inter-Rail cards are available from selected stations and travel agents.**

- **The Under 26 International Youth Card and the Euro<26 card provide members with discounted air fares worldwide, and also offers reductions on places to stay and visit.**

- **If you intend to travel by train in Britain, you can buy a Young Persons Railcard at a cost of £20 (2006 prices) which entitles you to a third off most ticket prices. Everyone aged 16-25 is eligible to have one, as are full-time students aged 26 and over. You can buy the Railcard at large stations, some travel agents and from student services at college or by phone. See contacts.**

COMPLAINTS

If your train (or bus) is late, there's not a lot in law that you can do about it. When you buy a ticket, you have no legal guarantee that the train will run on time (or even at all), or that you'll have a seat when it does come. All this is explained in the small print, known as the conditions of carriage, which can be checked at station ticket offices.

You may be offered compensation if you're stuck on a train or Goldline Express Bus that has been seriously delayed.

If you have a complaint about a train service, you can ask for a complaints form at a station or contact Translink Customer Care Coordinator.

■ BRIEF CASE: Emma

Emma bought a ticket for a day trip to London, saying that she wanted to travel on the next train, leaving in 15 minutes. When the inspector checked her ticket on the train, she asked Emma to pay a further £6, as she had been undercharged by the booking clerk. Although Emma claimed that it was the train operating company's mistake in selling her the wrong ticket, by law she had to pay the difference. When a contract is made, one side cannot gain by the other side's genuine mistake.

Getting started

The licence

It is an offence to drive or ride a motor vehicle without the correct licence. You are entitled to a full driving licence when you have passed your test, and the licence will be valid for ten years renewable until you are 70. Licences for drivers over 70 are issued for three years at a time. You must display amber 'R' plates for one year after you have passed your test. A vehicle displaying these must not exceed 45mph.

New licences are now the size of a credit card and contain the holder's photograph. You must advise any change of address immediately - or risk a fine.

If you want to learn to drive, you need a provisional driving licence. Application forms are available from post offices, local vehicle licensing offices and directly from DVLNI. When you get your licence, sign it immediately.

Learning to drive a car

When you are driving on a provisional licence you must display 'L' plates, which should be removed or covered up when the vehicle is not being driven by a learner. You must not drive on a motorway, and must have someone with you in the front passenger seat who is over 21 and has held a full Northern Ireland, Great Britain or EU driving licence for three years. This person must be fit to drive and must not have had more than the legal amount of alcohol.

The driving test is in two parts, a written theory exam and a practical test. You need to pass the theory test before taking the practical test. During the theory test, you will be asked to answer 35 multiple-choice questions in 40 minutes and then, you will watch 14 short video clips to identify hazards which might lead you to change speed or direction. The practical test lasts about an hour.

Learning to ride a motorcycle, moped or scooter

Motorcyclists also have to take a theory paper and a practical test to gain a licence. A full car or motorcycle licence allows you to ride a moped (with an engine of up to 50cc and a maximum speed of no more than 50kph) without 'L' plates. A full car licence or a provisional motorcycle licence allows you to ride a motorcycle up to 125cc and 11kw with 'L' plates.

Motorcyclists must learn on a machine no larger than 125cc. If you pass your test on a motorcycle between 75cc and 120cc, you may ride any motorcycle up to 125cc. If you pass your test on a motorcycle between 120cc and 125cc you will be given a standard motorcycle licence and after passing the practical test, you will be restricted for two years to bikes with a power output of up to 25kw, after which you may ride any size of bike.

Learner motorcyclists may not ride on a motorway, nor carry a pillion passenger. Mopeds, scooters, and motorised skateboards cannot be used on the public roads without a licence, road tax and insurance.

use the law with care try talking first

MOT

Most vehicles that are four or more years old must pass an 'MOT' test if they are to be used or left on the road.

Road tax

A car or motorbike must display a current tax disc, whether it is being used or just standing on the public road. The fine for breaking this regulation is normally about twice the cost of the disc. The Driving and Vehicle Licensing Northern Ireland (usually known as DVLNI), now has powers to wheel clamp and remove vehicles not currently taxed, and to charge a fee for their release. It is a crime to use a tax disc belonging to another vehicle.

If you have a vehicle that you take off the road (e.g. for repairs) and decide not to tax, you must inform DVLNI on the reminder form sent to you when the vehicle licence is due for renewal. The penalty for not doing this is a fine of up to £1,000.

Insurance

It is an offence to use a motor vehicle on the road without insurance. The penalties for this are very heavy. Failure to have insurance means a fine and penalty points on a licence, and possible disqualification.

It is also an offence for someone to allow their car or motorcycle to be used by a person who is not insured to drive it.

There are three different kinds of motor insurance, offering different levels of cover:

- **if the road traffic collision is your fault, third party insurance only pays for damage caused to other people or their property (and not to your own vehicle). This is the minimum level of insurance cover required by law;**
- **third party fire and theft gives you further protection by covering your vehicle against theft or fire damage;**
- **fully comprehensive insurance is usually the most expensive, but covers the cost of repairing accident damage to your vehicle as well as compensating you and others for injuries or damage in the collision.**

When you apply for any insurance, make sure the information you give is accurate and complete. If it's not, your insurance will be invalid. It's an offence knowingly to make a false statement to obtain insurance. For more information, see **money**, page 58.

■ BRIEF CASE: Sarah

Sarah bought a Morgan sports car, and insured it for her and her fiancé to drive. The car, worth £26,000, was stolen. When she claimed on her insurance, it came to light that her fiancé had received a serious motoring conviction several years ago, which Sarah had failed to mention on the application form. The insurance policy was therefore not valid, and Sarah received no compensation for the loss of her car.

cars and motorbikes

AT WHAT AGE?

At 16 you can ride a moped up to 50cc, a small tractor, mowing machine or invalid car. If you receive a disability living allowance, at the higher rate, you can also drive a car.

At 17 you can drive a car with up to 8 passenger seats, a motor tricycle, a motorbike up to 125cc, a large tractor and a van or lorry up to 3.5 tons.

At 18 you can drive a van or lorry up to 7.5 tons.

At 21 you can drive all other vehicles. For hiring a car, most car hire companies have a minimum age of 21 or 23.

Traffic offences

Every vehicle on the road must meet a whole set of regulations covering brakes, tyres, lights, mirrors, steering and even windscreen washer bottles (which must, by law, never be empty). A police officer may stop a vehicle at any time to check that it is in roadworthy condition, and it is no excuse for the driver to claim that they didn't realise a light wasn't working. These are absolute offences and apply even if the driver was completely unaware of the problem.

If the police believe a vehicle is not roadworthy, they can instruct the driver to get it checked and repaired by a garage (usually within 14 days), give the driver a fixed penalty or call up a specially trained vehicle examiner to inspect the car or bike there and then. A police officer who feels a vehicle is so dangerous that someone will probably be injured if it is used any further, can immediately ban it from being driven.

Cycling

Cyclists are expected to follow the same basic laws as other road users. They have a duty of care to pedestrians, other riders and road users. It is against the law to carry a passenger (unless the bike has been built or adapted for the purpose) and to pass the stop line when the traffic lights are red.

It is an offence to ride under the influence of alcohol or drugs. There is no breath test for cyclists; a court would instead be guided by evidence from the officer who made the arrest.

BUYING A CAR

• A small popular car is usually less of a risk. Spare parts are cheaper and easier to obtain, insurance costs lower and it will probably be easier to sell when you want to change it.

• A car bought privately is usually cheaper than one bought from a dealer, but you have fewer rights if things go wrong. The *Sale of Goods Act 1979* (see money, page 48), gives greater protection if you buy from a dealer. A car bought privately need only be "as described". The legal expression "caveat emptor" (meaning "buyer beware"), particularly applies when buying a second-hand car. It is notoriously difficult to get problems sorted out once you have paid for the car.

• Look at the car in daylight. Take someone along with you who knows about cars. Check the owner's purchase documents to see if any hire-purchase payments are still due. For between £100-£300 the RAC, AA or Green Flag will inspect and report on the mechanical state of the car, check on the HP payments and tell you whether the car has been stolen or is an insurance write-off. AA Car Data provide a similar service at a slightly lower cost, without the mechanical inspection.

• Look to see if the car's mileage tallies with the MOT certificate and the service history. You can also check with previous owners. Ask the dealer if they have tried to verify the mileage - they have to do this by law. Be wary if there is a sticker on the speedometer indicating that there is no guarantee that the mileage is accurate.

• Ask to see the Vehicle Registration Document (V5)(C)NI. If it's a private sale, it should contain the seller's name and address. It also gives the Vehicle Identification Number (VIN), which should correspond with the number stamped on identification plates under the bonnet and on the floor. If you have any doubts, leave the car alone.

• If you buy a car that turns out to be stolen, it remains the property of the true owner - meaning that you will almost certainly lose your money, unless you can get it back from the person from whom you bought the car.

■ BRIEF CASE: Anna

Anna went to look at a Ford Focus, advertised privately in her local paper. She asked the seller if the car had been in an accident. He said no, but having bought the car, Anna later found evidence of major crash repairs. She went back to the seller, pointed out the car was not as described and eventually got her money back. However, if the car had just been unreliable (even breaking down on her first drive), there is probably little she could have done, as there is nothing in law that states that a car bought privately must be of satisfactory or reasonable quality.

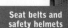

Safety

Seat belts and safety helmets

Seat belts (front and rear), where fitted, must be worn by drivers and passengers. If a passenger in your car does not wear a belt, it is he or she who will be prosecuted, not you - unless the passenger is under 14, when it is your responsibility.

Motorcyclist and pillion passengers must both wear an approved safety helmet on all journeys. This regulation does not apply to a follower of the Sikh religion while he is wearing a turban. Dark visors may not be worn at night or when visibility is poor. Only visors stamped with the British Kitemark BS 4110 or ECE 22-05 or equivalent standards are legal for road use.

SPEED LIMITS

Cars and motorcycles are limited to
- **30 mph in built-up areas, unless marked otherwise,**
- **60 mph on single carriageways,**
- **70 mph on dual carriageways and motorways.**

Speed limits are lower for buses, lorries, and cars towing trailers.

Speeding

Speeding is an absolute offence, which means that it is no defence to say that it wasn't dangerous or that you didn't realise that you were breaking the speed limit. Nor is there much point in denying that you were travelling at the speed the police say you were, unless you can prove it. You will usually be fined and given penalty points.

If you break the speed limit, or are seen by the police to be driving carelessly or dangerously, you must be warned of the possibility of prosecution at the time of the offence or served with a summons within 14 days of the offence. Otherwise you cannot be convicted, unless a collision occurred at the time or immediately after.

Driving badly

Careless driving is to drive in a way that is not how a careful and reasonable driver would behave. Pulling out from a side road without looking is an example of this.

Dangerous driving is to drive in a way that is dangerous to people or property, such as driving very fast through a built-up area or overtaking on a sharp bend. Dangerous driving and causing death by dangerous driving are very serious offences, which courts will punish with fines, disqualification, and imprisonment. If you face such a charge, get in touch with a solicitor straightaway.

Stolen vehicles

Stealing a vehicle to sell on to someone else is theft. Joy-riding, or taking a car to ride around in and then dumping it, is a different offence known as "taking a vehicle without the owner's consent" or TWOC. Both are punishable by a fine or imprisonment.

In the *Criminal Justice (NI) Order 2004*, aggravated vehicle-taking carries a sentence of up to five years' imprisonment, a fine or both. Another more serious offence of causing death or grievous bodily injury by aggravated vehicle taking carries a sentence of up to 14 years, a fine or both.

Mobile phones

It is an offence to use a hand held mobile phone when driving. Motorists can be fined from £30 to £1,000 and it is proposed that penalty points will be given from early 2007.

use the law with care try talking first

■ BRIEF CASE: Peter

Peter was involved in a crash with a motorcycle. He feared that it was his fault and that he would lose his licence, as he already had a number of penalty points. He persuaded his wife Sophie, who was not in the car at the time, to tell the police that it was she who was driving. A week later they both admitted the deception, but were charged with perverting the course of justice. Peter and Sophie were sentenced to four and two months in prison.

Drinking and driving

Alcohol seriously affects a driver's judgement and reactions. There is no law that limits a driver to a certain number of drinks, such as two pints of beer or one glass of wine, but there is a maximum amount of alcohol that you may have in your body while driving or being in charge of a car. In law, being in charge of a car includes simply sitting in the driving seat of a parked car.

The limits The amount of alcohol in a person's body can be measured in their breath, blood, or urine. A driver will be found guilty of drink-driving if they have more than 35 micrograms of alcohol in 100 ml of breath, 80 mg of alcohol in 100 ml of blood, or more than 107 mg of alcohol in 100 ml of urine.

Breath tests Uniformed police can breathalyse anyone whom they reasonably suspect of driving with alcohol in their body; or who has committed a traffic offence or been involved in an accident, however minor, even if there is no suspicion of alcohol. A uniformed police officer is entitled to stop motorists where there is a reasonable suspicion that they have consumed any alcohol and ask them to take a breath test.

If the test is positive or the driver refuses a breath test, the driver will be arrested and taken to a police station for further tests.

No escape A driver who fails to blow into the device properly, or refuses to take a test, will still end up with a heavy fine and have his or her licence endorsed with three to eleven penalty points. Courts rarely accept that there are special reasons for drivers being over the limit. Disqualification from driving is almost automatic. A person whose driving was impaired by alcohol and who causes someone's death may be sent to prison for up to 14 years and will be disqualified from driving for at least 2 years.

■ BRIEF CASE: Paul

Paul had had a few drinks when he was phoned by a friend who had run out of petrol, miles from anywhere, with his old and sick mother. Paul got into his car to go and fetch them, but was stopped by the police and breathalysed positive. Although he told the court that it was an emergency, the magistrates still found Paul guilty of drinking and driving, saying that the police, RAC or AA could instead have been called to help.

99% PROOF

101

Penalty points Courts deal with most motoring offences through a system of penalty points that are entered on a driver's licence. Anyone receiving twelve or more points within a period of three years will almost always be disqualified from driving for at least six months. Details of the points carried for each offence are given in the Highway Code for Northern Ireland. Drivers who have six or more penalty points on their licence within two years of their test, go back to being a learner until they pass a further test.

road traffic collisions

What to do Accidents happen to the most careful of drivers, often through no fault of their own. If you are involved in a collision, there are certain things that you should and should not do....

- Stop immediately. Try to stay calm, even if people are yelling and screaming at you.
- Check that everyone involved is OK. If anyone is injured, call an ambulance before you do anything else.
- You must give your name and address and details of your vehicle to anyone who has reasonable need to know them. This includes a police officer at the scene of the collision, anyone who is injured, anyone whose property is damaged and the owner of any animal injured or killed. If someone is injured, you must also produce your insurance certificate to show that you are properly insured. If you can't do this at the time of the accident, then you must give this information to the police as soon as possible. If you don't, you will be committing an offence.
- Make sure you get the name, address, vehicle registration number and insurance details of the other drivers involved.
- Contact your insurance company as soon as possible, and also make a detailed note of everything that happened. This should cover the time of day, weather, light, estimated speeds, position of vehicles before and after the accident, what people said and anything else that you think might be relevant. If you can, take photos before anything is moved, or draw a sketch plan as soon as you feel able to do so.
- Don't drive away without stopping. It is a criminal offence.
- Be cautious if the other driver suggests not calling the police and offers you cash to cover the damage. It might be an offence not to report the collision, and you may find that the damage to your vehicle costs a lot more than you are being offered. If someone is injured in the accident it is an offence not to report it to the police.
- Don't admit it was your fault. You may find later that the other driver was drunk, driving too fast, or without lights - in which case you might not be to blame at all. If you do admit responsibility, your words may end up by being used against you in court and may affect your insurance claim.

police
and courts

young citizen's **passport**

INDIVIDUALS ENGAGING IN SOCIETY *Citizenship Foundation*

powers and duties

Powers and duties

Most of the information that the police receive comes from the general public. Without this help their work would be much more difficult.

Much of the law setting out police powers and duties when investigating crime is contained in the *Police and Criminal Evidence (NI) Order 1989*. As part of this, the government publishes guidelines that the police must follow when searching for and collecting evidence. These are guidelines that indicate how police officers should carry out things such as stopping, searching and questioning suspects. If they are broken when the police are, say, questioning a suspect, a judge or magistrate may decide that the evidence obtained cannot be used in court, and the police officers concerned may be disciplined.

Copies of the Codes of Practice are available from libraries and at every police station. Anyone questioned by the police has a right to read them.

Special powers Under the UK-wide provisions of the *Terrorism Act 2000* and the *Anti-Terrorism, Crime and Security Act 2001*, the police have special powers to deal with terrorism and some other serious offences. They can only be used in limited circumstances, but when they are, they give police increased powers to search and detain suspects.

In Northern Ireland, the police and army are given additional search and detention powers under the temporary provisions of the *Terrorism Act 2000* to deal with paramilitarism. There is also a different system of trial for those who commit "scheduled" (ie terrorist related) offences. This is commonly known as the Diplock system, named after the judge who recommended it. It is very controversial because such trials take place in front of a single judge without a jury.

POLICE DISCIPLINE

Police officers must obey both the law of the land, and their own code of discipline. This discipline code is broken if an officer:
- **unreasonably neglects their duty;**
- **makes a false written or spoken statement;**
- **misuses their authority, e.g. through unnecessary violence;**
- **is rude or abusive;**
- **is racially discriminatory.**

The Police have a legal duty to promote racial equality and good relations between people of different racial groups

stop and search

Stop!

If a police officer stops you in the street, you are entitled to know the officer's name and the police station where they work. You are also entitled to know why the officer has stopped you. It is not acceptable for this to be simply because of your colour, dress, hairstyle or the fact that you might have been in trouble before.

Strictly speaking, you don't have to answer a police officer's questions, but someone who refuses to give their name and address may well find themselves arrested if the officer believes that they have something to hide.

use the law with care **try talking first**

However, if the police suspect that you have committed (or are about to commit) an arrestable offence - such as theft, assault or carrying an offensive weapon - then you must give your name and address, but need not say any more. You have the right not to answer any more questions until you have received legal advice, see page 107.

Stay calm 1 If you're stopped by the police, keep calm and don't overreact. If you're obstructive and rude, you're more likely to be arrested. Staying calm will also help you remember what happened and what was said. If you deliberately mislead the police by giving false information or wasting their time, you risk a fine or imprisonment.

Search!

People

The police can search anyone (or the vehicles they have travelled in) who has been arrested or is suspected of carrying:

- **illegal drugs;**
- **stolen goods or goods on which duty has not been paid;**
- **weapons, or anything that might be used as a weapon; or**
- **anything that might be used for theft, burglary, deception, joyriding or the hunting or poaching of animals as well as people suspected of involvement in other sorts of criminal activity, such as terrorist acts.**

Any search involving more than a check of your outer clothing should be done out of public view or in a police station or van. If the search requires more than the removal of outer clothing, it should be done by someone of the same sex. The way the search is carried out can depend on what the police are looking for. For example, the police may decide to make an intimate search of someone suspected of carrying drugs - given the possibility that the drugs are being hidden inside the person's body.

Stay calm 2 If you, or the vehicle in which you are travelling, are searched by the police, the officer should state beforehand why the search is taking place and what they expect to find. You have every right to ask for an explanation if this has not been made clear.

If the police search you illegally, they are committing an assault. But if they have good reason, and you refuse, you may be charged with obstruction.

The police should normally make a written record of the search and tell you. You can ask for a copy at any time within the next year.

Property The police do not have the power to enter and search any house or building that they choose. But they are allowed to carry out a search if:

- **they have the agreement of the occupier of the building; or**
- **they have reason to believe they might find someone who has committed an arrestable offence, or to look for relevant evidence in a property that was controlled by someone before they were arrested; or**
- **they have a warrant (or permission) from a court; or**
- **in order to catch an escaped prisoner, save life, prevent serious property damage or to prevent certain kinds of disturbance.**

If possible, the police should explain why they are making the search and should keep a record of whether they needed to use force to get in, any damage caused, and anything they took away. If the search is unlawful, it may be possible to get compensation, but this is not easy.

arrest

When the police make an arrest, they are taking the person under the care and control of the law. This means that for the time being, the suspect loses certain freedoms - such as to go and do as they please - but, in return, has certain rights designed to protect them from unreasonable treatment.

If you are arrested and taken to a police station, you are entitled to a:

- **know the reason for your arrest;**
- **see a solicitor;**
- **have someone told where you are;**
- **read a copy of the Codes of Practice, which explain the procedures the police should follow when questioning you.**

You should be given a written note of these rights and cautioned - see page 107.

You can be held by the police if they do not have enough evidence to charge you and they reasonably believe that they can preserve or obtain further evidence by continuing to question you.

You cannot normally be held for more than 24 hours without being charged or released. If a serious offence is being investigated, a senior police officer can authorise your detention for a further twelve hours, which can be extended up to a total of 96 hours with the approval of a magistrates' court.

HELPING THE POLICE WITH THEIR ENQUIRIES

If you are asked to go to a police station to help with enquiries, it's important to know if you are being arrested, or whether the decision to attend is up to you. If you are being asked to go voluntarily, you may refuse - although the police may then decide to arrest you - and then you have to go.

You are entitled to send a message to your family or a friend telling them where you are, and to receive free legal advice from a solicitor, even though you are attending the police station voluntarily.

If you have not been arrested and go to the police station voluntarily, you may leave at any time you wish.

use the law with care try talking first

Legal advice

In almost all circumstances, anyone who has been arrested, or who goes to a police station voluntarily, is entitled to legal advice from the solicitor on duty or one of their own choice. The consultation with the duty solicitor is free and in private.

If you have been arrested or are being questioned about a serious arrestable offence, or if you feel at all unsure about your legal position, it is better not to answer questions (except your name and address) until you have had a chance to speak to a solicitor.

With the approval of a senior officer, the police can delay access to a solicitor chosen by the detained person (but not to the duty solicitor) for up to 36 hours if this might interfere with the evidence, endanger or alert others or hinder the recovery of property obtained as a result of the offence.

Questioning

The police should not normally interview a person under 18, or anyone suffering from a mental disorder without a parent or an "appropriate adult" present. An appropriate adult can be a parent, guardian or relative; a social worker; or failing these some other responsible adult.

If you have been arrested, you must give the police your name and address, but you have the right after that to stay silent and not answer any further questions. However, the court will be told of this if the case goes to trial, and it may strengthen the case against you. If you refuse to answer questions in court, the magistrates or jury are allowed to take this into account in deciding whether you are guilty.

The Patten Report, which was drafted as a result of the *1998 Belfast Agreement* emphasises the importance of training all police in standards of human rights. It recommends that all new and existing officers should take an oath committing themselves to uphold human rights in all aspects of their job. There are clear rules governing the way police officers can question a person, which are designed to stop unfair pressure being placed on a suspect.

There should be regular breaks for food and the cell and interview room should be clean, properly heated, ventilated, and lit. Someone who is deaf or has difficulty in understanding English should be given a signer or an interpreter.

If, after questioning, the police decide to arrest you, they should give you written information about your legal rights.

The caution

Once a police officer has reason to believe that you have committed an offence, they will usually caution you by saying: "You do not have to say anything, but I must caution you that if you do not mention when questioned something that you later rely on in court, it may harm your defence. If you do say anything it may be given in evidence." In some cases it would be impractical to issue this caution immediately, in which case it should be issued as soon as possible.

Tape recording Your interview at the police station will normally be recorded on tape. The officer will begin with questions about your name and address.

If the interview is not recorded, notes should be made by the officer concerned. You should normally have the opportunity to see these notes and to sign them if you agree that they are a fair record of what was said.

Fingerprints and photographs The police can take fingerprints of anyone who gives their consent or in certain circumstances without their consent. If the person doesn't co-operate, reasonable force can be used. The police are generally allowed to photograph people charged with a recordable offence but must not use force. Fingerprints and photographs must be destroyed if the person is charged and found not guilty, or not charged at all (unless they admit the offence and are formally cautioned for it, or in the case of photographs, if the person has a previous conviction for a recordable offence).

charge, caution, release

After questioning you, the police must decide what to do next. If there appears to be enough evidence, they can:

- **charge you with the offence and send the papers to the Public Prosecution Service (PPS) who will then decide whether to continue with the case; or**
- **report you to the PPS for them to decide whether the evidence is sufficient to prosecute you.**

In either event the PPS will, in appropriate cases, consider alternative ways of dealing with cases involving young persons under 18, e.g. by way of an informed warning, caution or Youth Conference.

Charged If you are to be charged, you will be given a charge sheet indicating the nature of the offence, when and where you are due to appear in court and the conditions of your bail.

Once you are charged you should not be asked any further questions except in certain specified situations, for example, when new information has come to light.

Bail If you are charged with an offence, the law states that you should normally be released on bail - unless the police believe you should be held:

- **because they doubt the truth of the name and address that you have given;**
- **for the protection of others, to stop you committing another offence or to stop you interfering in other investigations;**
- **for your own protection (or, if you are under 18, because it is in your own interests); or**
- **to make sure you turn up in court.**

If you are not released by the police, you must be brought before a magistrate at the earliest opportunity, who will decide whether you can be released on bail and, if so, what conditions should apply. For example, you may be required to report to the police station once a week, or to have someone provide a financial guarantee that you will be present in court when required. If the court refuses or applies conditions to bail it must give the reasons for this decision.

A person who is charged with, or already convicted of, murder, attempted murder, manslaughter, rape or attempted rape, will only be given bail if the court deciding the matter considers that there are exceptional circumstances which justify doing so. Courts also need not grant bail if it appears that the defendant was already on bail when the offence was committed.

A formal caution

This is a strong warning from a senior police officer reminding you that you could have been sent to court, and that if you commit further offences, that is almost certainly what will happen. Cautions are not for serious offences and can be given only if the accused admits guilt.

Youth Justice Agency

The Youth Justice Agency is responsible for the Youth Conference Service, the Juvenile Justice Centre and for schemes for the prevention of offending by children and young people in the community.

Youth conferencing

The Youth Conference Service organises restorative justice conferences between young offenders and their victims. These meetings are arranged either at the request of the Public Prosecutor or the Youth Court.

COMPLAINTS AGAINST THE POLICE

If you feel that you have suffered, or witnessed police misconduct, you may decide that you want to make an official complaint to the police ombudsman.

The police ombudsman aims to provide a free, independent, impartial police complaints system for both the people and police. The office investigates complaints about how the police behave when they are doing their job. Allegations against an officer may range from breaking the police code of conduct to serious criminal behaviour.

The police ombudsman cannot investigate complaints about the behaviour of an officer off-duty or complaints that are out of time. Further information on this and how to make a complaint is available from the Citizens Advice Bureau or the Office of the Police Ombudsman, see contacts.

The conference offers the victim the opportunity to tell the young offender of the harm caused by the crime and the offender the chance to face up to its impact and the opportunity to "clear up the mess."

Conferences can only take place if the offender admits to the offence and agrees to meet the victim and if the prosecutor considers it appropriate.

The conference is expected to identify a plan of action to prevent further offending and make amends to the victim. The young offender must agree to the contents of the plan.

These action plans become known as Diversionary Youth Conference Orders if approved by the prosecutor and Youth Conference Orders if approved by the court.

The Juvenile Justice Centre

Children between 10-17 years old, boys or girls whom the court believes should not be released on bail, may be remanded to the Juvenile Justice Centre until their case can be heard. A child may receive a Juvenile Justice Centre Order, which means he or she would be placed in custody for up to two years.

Community Services

Courts sometimes require offenders to carry out some kind of community service as part of their sentence. Sometimes this is an alternative to detention or imprisonment. A person receiving a Community Service Order, a Reparation Order or Community Responsibility Order will be required to undertake some kind of unpaid community work. In the case of a Reparation Order this will be designed to make good the damage caused by the offence.

A person who fails to carry out the requirements of the order is called back to court.

courts

The PPS

The Public Prosecution Service has the responsibility to decide whether criminal proceedings should be initiated or continued, against those accused of a crime in Northern Ireland, based on evidence provided by the police.

Charge or Summons

The date and time of your first appearance in court is stated on the police charge sheet or by summons through the post.

If you are 17 or under, your case will normally be heard in a youth court. If you are 18 or over, your first appearance will be in the local adult magistrates' court.

use the law with care try talking first

Youth court

If the accused is under 18, the case must normally be heard in a youth court.

If a young person is charged jointly with an adult the trial may be held in a magistrates' court or, in serious cases such as murder, in the Crown Court.

A youth court is made up of a resident magistrate and two lay magistrates (one of which is a woman), trained to deal with cases involving young people.

The parent or guardian of young people under 18 may be required to attend court.

Members of the public are not allowed in a youth court to listen to the case, nor can the identity or pictures of any young person concerned in the trial be published in the press.

Magistrates' court

All criminal cases pass through magistrates' courts, in some way or another. The court is presided over by a resident magistrate, sitting alone. A resident magistrate will reach a verdict and pass sentence on all cases involving less serious offences (known as summary offences). More serious cases are dealt with by the Crown Court, but before they reach this stage, it is the resident magistrates' job to decide whether there is enough evidence for the accused to stand trial. There are some offences that can be heard by either a magistrates' or Crown Court, and in certain circumstances the accused can decide which to choose.

Crown Court

This is the Court where more serious offences are heard. A judge takes charge of the hearing to make sure that the evidence is properly presented, but the verdict is reached by the jury. Where the accused is charged with a scheduled offence, ie a terrorist-type offence, the judge sits alone without a jury. The judge will pass sentence if the defendant is found guilty, and is generally able to impose higher sentences than a magistrates' court. The sentence is decided by taking into account any maximum set by law, the circumstances surrounding the case, previous convictions, and possibly the background of the defendant if it is thought to have any bearing on the case.

There are procedures set out to ensure that a young person accused of a crime is not made to feel intimidated by the experience and receives a fair trial.

courts

Age of criminal responsibility

A child under the age of ten who breaks the law cannot be charged with the crime. However, children under ten who are out of control may be given a child safety order (placing them under the supervision of a social worker) or a care order (taking them into care).

Northern Ireland Court Service

If you need to go to court, for example as a witness or a juror, and need information on what you can expect or what you might have to do, your local court should be able to help. Further details are available on the Northern Ireland Court Service website, see **contacts**.

Juries

The job of a jury, which sits in a Crown Court, is to decide on the facts of a criminal case and on the guilt or innocence of the accused. It is made up of twelve adults, aged between 18-70, who have lived in Northern Ireland for a continuous period of three months. They are chosen at random from the local Electoral Register (see page 120), but there are certain categories of people who cannot be selected. These include judges, magistrates, solicitors, barristers, ministers of religion, prison, police and probation officers, anyone on bail or who has been on probation within the last five years, anyone sentenced to prison, detention centre, youth custody or community service within the last ten years.

If you are called as a member of a jury, you will usually be given about six weeks' notice. Although some people, such as MPs, members of the armed forces and the medical profession have the right to be excused, normally it is compulsory. But if there is a strong reason why you are unable to serve - such as exams, a holiday which has been already booked, the care of a relative or major problems at work - then you may be excused or allowed to defer your service until later in the year, although it is important to make this clear as soon as possible.

Jurors are able to claim the cost of travel to Court and a small financial allowance. There is information for jurors on the Court Service websites, see **contacts**.

law, government
& human rights

young citizen's **passport**

INDIVIDUALS
ENGAGING IN
SOCIETY

Citizenship Foundation

Parliament

Between 30–50 major new laws are passed by Parliament in Westminster each year.

Starting as a Bill, each one must be debated and voted on by the House of Commons and the House of Lords before becoming law. The House of Lords can recommend changes and delay the progress of a Bill, but it can't actually stop it from being passed. The only Bill that the House of Lords can reject is one that tries to extend a Parliament's life beyond five years (the maximum time between general elections) - a protection against power being seized by a dictator.

After going through both Houses of Parliament, a Bill becomes an Act (or statute) by being given the royal assent by the Queen. Today this is a formality. The last monarch to refuse to approve an Act was Queen Anne in 1707.

Most Bills are put to Parliament by the Government as part of its overall policy. A small number are presented by individual MPs and peers, known as private members' Bills. Few of these become law, as there is only a limited amount of time to debate and vote on them. Most of Parliament's time is spent on Government business. Committees of MPs, known as Select Committees, monitor and question what Ministers and their departments do.

■ BRIEF CASE

brief case

A month after separating from his wife, a man broke into her parents house where she was staying and tried to have sex with her against her will. The husband was found guilty of attempted rape and sentenced to five years in prison. He appealed on the grounds that a husband could not be found guilty of raping his wife. The case went up to the House of Lords where it was heard by five senior judges. They decided that the rule that a husband could not rape his wife (which went back to before 1736) should no longer be part of the law, since a husband and wife were now seen as equal partners in marriage. As a result the law was changed and a man who forces his wife to have sexual intercourse against her will may now be guilty of rape.

European law

The UK is part of the European Union and has agreed to apply new laws agreed by the member states of the EU. This is explained on pages 132-133.

Courts

When a case comes to court, the magistrates or judge normally apply the law in the same way as courts have done in the past. This is called a system of precedent and ensures that similar cases are dealt with in a consistent way. However, there are times when the circumstances of a case have not arisen before, or when the senior judges decide that existing judgments do not reflect modern society. In these situations, by their decision, judges can create or change the law.

The Northern Ireland Assembly

Elections for the 108 members of the Northern Ireland Assembly (NIA) take place every five years. On 2 December 1999 power was devolved to the Assembly and its Executive Committee of Ministers. The Executive has twelve members; ten ministers each responsible for their own government department, presided over by the First and Deputy First Ministers. When devolution is in place the Assembly is responsible for all functions except for reserved matters, eg those relating to policing or criminal justice issues. Devolution was suspended on 14 October 2002 and replaced by direct rule from Westminster. The Secretary of State has assumed responsibility for all eleven government departments, assisted by a team of Northern Ireland Office ministers.

European Convention on Human Rights

This is an international agreement drawn up by the Council of Europe to protect people's human rights after the horrors of the Second World War. It took effect in 1953 and sets out fundamental rights and freedoms that everybody should have and the limited circumstances when the State may interfere with those freedoms. These include a right to liberty, a right to a fair trial, privacy, freedom of speech etc. The Council of Europe represents a wider group of countries than the EU.

Anyone who believes the law in this country has not dealt fairly with their rights can take their case to the European Court of Human Rights in Strasbourg. The UK has agreed to abide by the findings of the Strasbourg court but this is a long and costly process. Before the *Human Rights Act 1998* came into force the UK courts themselves had no power to deal with human rights cases.

Human rights law in Northern Ireland

Under the *Human Rights Act 1998,* the Northern Ireland Assembly, the Executive Committee, all Northern Ireland departments (including the Office of the First Minister and Deputy First Minister) and public bodies must follow the rights in the European Convention. This rule also applies during periods of suspension.

Judges in Northern Ireland have the power to rule out any laws passed by the NI Assembly, that break the Convention.

The Belfast Agreement established the Northern Ireland Human Rights Commission to protect and promote human rights in Northern Ireland. They have also been asked to consider the possibility of defining rights in a Bill of Rights for Northern Ireland. Most people consulted have supported the idea, but there is disagreement about what should be in it.

use the law with care try talking first

The Convention Rights in UK law

There are 16 basic rights in the *Human Rights Act*. They don't only affect matters of life and death like freedom from torture and killing; they also affect people's rights in everyday life: what they can say and do, their beliefs, their right to a fair trial and many other similar basic entitlements.

(Article 1 is introductory)

Article 2 Right to life

Everyone has the right to have their life protected by law. There are only certain very limited circumstances where it is acceptable for the state to take away someone's life, e.g. if a police officer acts justifiably in self-defence. The *Human Rights Act* has completely abolished the death penalty in the UK.

Article 3 Prohibition of torture

Everyone has the absolute right not to be tortured or subjected to treatment or punishment that is inhuman or degrading.

Article 4 Prohibition of slavery and forced labour

Everyone has the absolute right not to be treated as a slave or forced to perform certain kinds of labour.

Article 5 Right to liberty and security

Everyone has the right not to be deprived of their liberty – "arrested or detained" - except in limited cases specified in the Article (e.g. where they are suspected or convicted of committing a crime) and where this is justified by a clear legal procedure.

Human Rights Act 1998

In order to improve access to justice and the fairness of our laws and procedures, the *Human Rights Act 1998* was passed, incorporating into our law nearly all the rights contained in the Convention. Under this Act all our laws must, as far as possible, conform to the rights listed under the Convention, and public bodies – such as the armed forces, local authorities, schools, hospitals, the police, prisons and the courts – must carry out their work in a way that respects these basic human rights. If they don't, then the law or the actions of the public body can be challenged in our own courts. If a court says that an Act of Parliament is "incompatible" with the rights in the Convention, the Government can amend it quickly by using a special procedure.

human rights

Article 6 Right to a fair trial

Everyone has the right to a fair and public hearing within a reasonable period of time. This applies to both criminal charges and in sorting out cases concerning civil rights and obligations. Hearings must be by an independent and impartial tribunal established by law. It is possible to exclude the public from the hearing (though not the judgment) in order to protect national security or public order. Anyone facing a criminal charge is presumed innocent until proved guilty according to law and has certain minimum guaranteed rights to defend themselves.

Article 7 No punishment without law

Everyone normally has the right not to be found guilty of an offence arising out of actions which at the time they were committed were not criminal. There is also protection against later increases in the possible sentence for an offence.

Articles 8-11

The rights to the following freedoms (in Articles 8 to 11) may be restricted where this is necessary to protect things like public health or safety, the rights of others or to prevent crime (including racial offences).

  Interference with these rights that goes too far can be challenged in the courts who will try to strike a fair balance.

Article 8 Right to respect for private life

Everyone has the right to respect for their private and family life, their home and their correspondence.

Article 9 Freedom of thought, conscience and religion

Everyone is free to hold whatever views, beliefs and thoughts (including religious faith) they like.

Article 10 Freedom of expression

Everyone has the right to express their views on their own or in a group. This applies even if they are unpopular or disturbing. This right can be restricted in specified circumstances.

Article 11 Freedom of assembly and association

Everyone has the right to get together with other people in a peaceful way. They also have the right to associate with other people, which can include the right to form a trade union. These rights may be restricted only in specified circumstances.

Article 12 Right to marry

Men and women have the right to marry and start a family. Our national law still governs how and at what age this can take place.

(Article 13, which deals with legal remedies, is not incorporated into our law)

Article 14 Prohibition of discriminationn

Everyone has the right to benefit from these Convention rights regardless of race, religion, sex, political views or any other status, unless a restriction can be reasonably justified.

Article 1 of Protocol 1*
Protection of property

Everyone has the right to the peaceful enjoyment of their possessions. Public authorities cannot usually interfere with things we own or the way we use them, except in specified limited circumstances.

Article 2 of Protocol 1*
Right to education

Everyone has the right not to be denied access to the educational system.

Article 3 of Protocol 1*
Right to free elections

Elections must be free and fair, and take place by secret ballot. Some restrictions can be placed on those who are allowed to vote (e.g. a minimum age).

Articles 1 and 2 of Protocol 6*
Abolition of the death penalty

These provisions abolish the death penalty. There can be limited exceptions in times of war, but only in accordance with clearly specified laws.

* (a 'protocol' is a later addition to the Convention)

HOW DOES THE HUMAN RIGHTS ACT AFFECT US?

The Human Rights Act is a unique type of higher law, affecting all other laws. The rights and their limitations are a set of basic values. Respect for these rights and everything that goes with them may help change the way people think and behave. It should help create a society in which decisions and policies are better discussed and understood. But the freedoms protected by the Act are not a complete set of human values and do not, for example, include the right to work or freedom from poverty.

The Act cannot be used directly by one private individual against another. It is designed to indicate how judges in courts must interpret the law and how public bodies – such as the police, the prison service and local councils – must carry out their actions.

It protects fundamental freedoms – like liberty and free speech – but at the same time, allows limits to be placed on these rights in order to try to make sure that other people are also treated fairly.

For example, a person's right to liberty may be restricted if they are guilty of a serious crime. This is for other people's protection. Similarly there are limits placed on freedom of speech to prevent someone from shouting 'Fire!' in a crowded hall, when there isn't one.

voting and elections

You can vote at elections if you are at least 18 years of age and your name is on the Register of Electors.

You must be a citizen of Britain, the Irish Republic or the Commonwealth and resident in the UK. However citizens of other European Union countries who are resident in the UK are allowed to vote in European, Northern Ireland Assembly and local government elections.

In Northern Ireland, electors must have been resident in Northern Ireland for the whole of the three month period.

Registering to vote

The Electoral Register is usually published on 1 December each year. Two or three months before this, all those eligible to vote are required to complete an annual registration form, a copy of which is delivered to each household.

However you may add your name to the register after 1 December by completing a registration form available from your local Area Electoral Office, or downloading a copy from the Electoral Office Northern Ireland website, see **contacts**.

Identification

Voters in Northern Ireland are required to provide one of four forms of photographic identification before casting their vote. These are either:

- **a current Northern Ireland or Great Britain driving licence, or a Northern Ireland provisional driving licence, which bears the photograph of the holder; or**
- **a current UK or EU member state passport; or**
- **a current electoral identity card; or**
- **a Senior SmartPass.**

An electoral identity card is available from local Area Electoral Offices, see **contacts**.

Who can you vote for?

Most people standing in local, national or European elections represent a political party. All political parties have to be registered with the Electoral Commission. The party will then select its candidates for each election. Some people stand as an independent without belonging to any political party.

Local elections

The election of local councillors is held every four years, usually in the first week of May.

In Northern Ireland, local councils' responsibilities include: refuse collection and disposal, street cleaning, parks, cemeteries and leisure facilities.

As well as deciding how the services are to be run, local councillors also take up problems on behalf of those living in their area.

LOCAL COUNCILLOR, MLA, MP OR MEP?

You can stand for election as an MLA, MP or MEP if you are aged 21 or over and a British, Commonwealth or Irish Citizen. Citizens of other EU states may also stand as an MEP. If you want to be a local councillor you must either:

- have your name on the local electoral register; or
- rent or own land or property or

- have worked in the area for the last twelve months; or
- have lived in, or within three miles of, the area for the last twelve months.

Candidates standing as an MLA or MP must pay a deposit of £500, which they lose if they get less than five per cent of the votes cast. The deposit for MEPs is £5,000.

General elections

The election of all 646 MPs must take place at least every five years. Often, however, the party in power will call an election before this if it feels it will help its chances of gaining another term of office or, more rarely, because it has been defeated on a vital vote in the House of Commons and has lost the confidence of the House.

Most MPs represent a registered political party and each represents a defined area, called a constituency. The party with the greatest number of MPs forms the government, with the party leader becoming Prime Minister. If an MP dies or resigns, a by-election takes place to elect a new MP for the constituency.

Even if not a member of the Government, an MP can have influence by speaking in debates, talking to ministers and other MPs, and by trying to get a private member's Bill made law. MPs must represent everyone in their constituency.

Voting systems

Votes for general and by-elections in the United Kingdom are counted on a 'first past the post' system. People each cast one vote and the winning candidate is the one with the most votes. Elections to the Northern Ireland Assembly and the European Parliament follow a different system called proportional representation. Under this system, the number of seats that each party receives is roughly equal to their share of the votes. There is the possibility that the voting system for MPs will be changed to one of proportional representation. The Government has said that it plans to hold a vote or referendum on this.

European elections

At European elections we elect members of the European Parliament that meets both in Strasbourg (France) and Brussels (Belgium). They take place every five years. Most UK candidates belong to one of the main political parties and, if elected, join the MEPs of the 24 other countries in the European Union. MEPs sit in multinational political groups so for example, British Labour MEPs belong to the Party of European Socialists, along with socialists from the other EU states.

MEPs help to make European law by examining and commenting on proposals made by the European Commission (see **the european union** pages 132-133).

Campaigning

If you feel strongly about something and want to get involved yourself, a library, Citizens Advice Bureau, or one of the organisations or websites listed in the **contacts** section can probably give you some of the information you need to find out who to contact.

This ranges from individual action to something more co-ordinated, as a member of a group. Letter writing is the usual starting point - do your research, send it to a named person (the most senior within the organisation), keep a copy, and try to get others involved as well. If you can get a letter published in a newspaper, many more will know about your views, but do give your name and address - although you can ask the paper not to publish it.

Writing to your councillor, MLA, MP or MEP

If your problem is local, contact your local councillor through the council office. MLAs, MPs or MEPs can best take up problems for which the Government or European Union are responsible. Most MLAs, MPs and some MEPs have local 'surgeries' for which no appointment is necessary. They are often held on a Saturday, and advertised in the local paper. You can also write to your MLA or MEP locally and your MP at the House of Commons. Addresses are obtainable from the local library, and are listed under Member of Parliament in the business section of the phone book. Many MPs also have their own websites.

Protest

The same laws apply to people taking part in political action as any other area of life. Criminal damage, theft, assault etc. remain crimes - no matter how good the cause.

Demonstrations and marches are controlled by the *Public Order (NI) Order 1987* and the *Criminal Justice and Public Order (NI) 1998*. Organisers must inform the local police where and when the march will take place and how many people will be involved. If the police believe the demonstration is likely to disrupt seriously the life of the community, a senior police officer can issue a ban for a period of up to three months.

Trespassing

The *Criminal Justice and Public Order Act 1994* introduced the offence of aggravated trespass. It was aimed at hunt saboteurs, but can affect anyone who causes disruption to people going about their lawful business. It is an offence to trespass on private land in order to intimidate, obstruct or disrupt people who are behaving lawfully.

Complaining

If you have a complaint about something you have bought or a service you have received, it's important to act quickly. Some companies, and many public services, have special procedures for dealing with complaints. If it's a public service, such as a hospital or benefits agency, you can ask to see a copy of their charter which shows the level of service you are entitled to expect. If your complaint is not dealt with properly, think about contacting your local councillor or MP, particularly if your problem is over a public service.

- **act as quickly as possible,**
- **think carefully about what you want to achieve and if necessary get advice;**
- **make sure you talk or write directly to a person - such as the manager or director of services - who has the authority to deal with your complaint;**
- **always find out the name of the person you are talking to;**
- **keep a record of phone calls or letters that you send;**
- **stick to the facts, and work out how the law can help you;**
- **state clearly what you want to be done, set a reasonable time within which this should happen, and get back in touch if they haven't met the deadline.**

If you are still unhappy with the way your problem has been handled, you may be able to take your case to an Ombudsman. See **contacts**, General.

Judicial review

If a public body - like a government department, local authority, or hospital - makes a decision which actually seems to be fundamentally unfair , you can apply to have that decision reviewed in the High Court. Known as judicial review, it's a way of having illegal or unreasonable decisions changed. Examples of this have been when people have questioned a hospital's right to withhold an operation in a genuinely urgent case.

A judicial review can normally be started only when all other avenues of complaint have been exhausted. It's a very complicated and expensive process and so, before doing anything, it's important to get advice from a solicitor who understands this area of law.

the european
union

young citizen's **passport**

INDIVIDUALS
ENGAGING IN
SOCIETY

Citizenship Foundation

membership

Twenty-five countries are currently members of the European Union (EU).

Austria, Belgium, Cyprus, the Czech Republic, Denmark, Estonia, Finland, France, Germany, Greece, Hungary, Ireland, Italy, Latvia, Lithuania, Luxembourg, Malta, the Netherlands, Poland, Portugal, Slovakia, Slovenia, Spain, Sweden, and the United Kingdom.

Bulgaria and Romania are likely to join in 2007, and it is expected that negotiations will also begin with Turkey and Croatia.

Origins

After the end of the Second World War, governments throughout Europe were determined not to repeat the horrors of the War, in which 50 million people had died.

In 1951, France, Belgium, Italy, Luxembourg, the Netherlands, and West Germany signed an agreement setting up the European Coal and Steel Community through which the coal and steel production of all six countries came under the control of a single European authority.

The architects of this plan believed that placing coal and steel production outside the control of individual states would greatly reduce the likelihood of another war. Britain was invited to join the ECSC, but declined.

In the early years co-operation was mainly designed to make it easier for member states to trade with one another. Gradually, the scope of the union has widened, and covers many areas today, including employment, the environment, transport, travel, foreign policy – and for twelve of the member states a common currency – the euro.

use the law with care **try talking first**

The idea of European states forming a single market has always been central to the development of the European Union.

A single market means that goods, services, people, and money must be able to move freely between member states.

Over the last 30 years member states have agreed all kinds of measures to make this possible:

- **taxes and duties on products have been made broadly similar between member states,**
- **technical and safety specifications of goods have been standardised, so that goods made in one state meet the standards required in another,**
- **people are allowed to travel, live, study, and work more-or-less wherever they wish.**

A single currency

The EU has also eased the movement of goods and people through the creation of a single currency, also sometimes called economic and monetary union (EMU).

The idea was first proposed in 1969, but the first significant steps were not taken until around 1990 when member states interested in moving towards a single currency began to prepare their economies for this process.

They were required to meet a number of conditions – usually described as convergence criteria – such as having low interest rates, keeping currency rates and prices stable and keeping government expenditure within certain limits.

The Euro

On 1st January 2002, after a transition period of two years, twelve of the then fifteen EU member states moved to a single currency – the euro (€).

Since 28th February 2002, euro banknotes and coins have been the sole legal tender within these twelve countries.

The seven euro notes, from €5 - €500 are the same throughout the single currency area. Each country produces its own coins, of smaller value, although these can be used anywhere within the euro area, regardless of national origin.

The UK and the Euro

The United Kingdom, Denmark, and Sweden decided not to proceed with the single currency. Denmark has held two national referendums on joining the euro, rejecting the idea on both occasions. In 2003, the people of Sweden voted against the euro. The UK government has also undertaken to hold a referendum on the issue when the government believes that its own five convergence criteria have been met.

Measures have been gradually introduced to help people move around the EU as easily as possible.

Travel

Citizens of an EU member state have the right to travel to any EU country, if they have a valid passport or identity card. This right may be restricted only for reasons of public order, public security, or public health.

EU citizens also have the right to travel within the EU with members of their family, but if they do not have EU nationality they may be required to have a visa, in addition to their passport.

Border controls

There are no customs checks for people travelling from one EU member state to another – although police controls on some frontiers remain, checking for terrorist activity, drug-trafficking and organised crime.

In addition, identity checks for EU citizens, have been abolished at many borders under what is called the Schengen Agreement. This allows people to travel from one country to another without having their passport or identity documents examined. All member states except the UK and Ireland have joined this group.

Health care

Citizens of EU member states who fall ill within another EU country are entitled to emergency treatment under that country's health scheme.

The treatment is free to someone who lives in Northern Ireland who can show the medical authorities their

European Health Insurance Card.

A person who doesn't have an EHIC is still entitled to treatment but may be asked to pay its full cost.

Help

An EU citizen who gets into difficulties in a country outside the EU may seek protection from the embassy or consulate of any EU member state.

For example, a British student arrested in a Russian city without a British consular office is entitled to help from the Swedish or Finnish consulate.

use the law with care try talking first

Work

British and Irish citizens are entitled to work in any EU country, and should be offered employment under the same conditions as citizens of that state. It would be against the law, for example, for an Italian firm to require Irish job applicants to have higher qualifications than their Italian counterparts – and vice versa.

Most jobs are open to all EU citizens. However, member states are allowed to insist that only nationals of that state hold certain public service posts, such as those in the police or armed forces. A residence permit is required for anyone who wants to stay in another member state for more than three months. This requires ID, if they don't have a paid job, and evidence of financial support.

Conditions

Generally speaking, a British or Irish citizen working in an EU member state has exactly the same employment rights and duties as everyone else in that country, and it is against the law for that person to be discriminated against on grounds of their nationality.

A British or Irish worker in Berlin, for example, should receive the same pay, employment opportunities, and health and safety protection as his or her German counterparts.

Qualifications

The EU operates on the system that someone qualified to work in a particular profession in their own country is also able to carry out that work in any other member state. However not all qualifications are automatically recognised – and applicants may need to check whether their particular diploma or certificate is recognised.

Benefits

Citizens of EU member states are entitled to the same welfare and social security benefits as nationals of the country in which they are working. This covers sickness and maternity benefits, benefits for accidents at work and unemployment. They also have the same rights, where it is available, to accommodation, such as local authority housing.

Taxes

A person who lives and works in an EU member state must normally pay taxes in the same way as any other resident of that country. Levels of taxation vary from one EU state to another, but work is under way to try to find ways of harmonising taxation across member states.

goods

Customs duties

Generally speaking, goods purchased by people for their own use may be bought in other member states and brought back to Northern Ireland without having to pay extra tax or duties. The few exceptions include new cars, boats, and aeroplanes.

People can bring in as much tobacco and alcohol from other EU member states as they like, as long as it is for personal use only and not for resale. But there is a limit of 200 cigarettes if travelling from the Czech Republic, Estonia, Hungary, Latvia, Lithuania, Poland, Slovakia and Slovenia. Customs officials in the UK have the right to stop people and check this, and to confiscate any items they believe are not for personal use.

The structure of the government of the European Union is not easy to understand - possibly because there are several organisations that help to determine EU policy.

THE EUROPEAN COUNCIL

The European Council is the name given to the regular meetings between the heads of the member states. They decide the issues the European Union should be concerned with. In the past this has included unemployment, drug trafficking, and enlarging the EU.

The Council of Ministers The Council of Ministers is one of the most influential bodies in the EU. It consists of government ministers from each member state with powers to adopt new laws, take decisions about how the EU is run, recommend policy, and negotiate with non-member states on behalf of the EU. It's at the centre government in the EU, rather like the Cabinet is in the UK.

Decisions Until the mid 1980s, decisions by the Council of Ministers tended to have to be unanimous. If a nation disagreed, the measure could not be passed. Today the Council generally uses a system called qualified majority voting. Each member state has a certain number of votes, broadly reflecting the size of the country in terms of its population.

For example, France, Germany, Italy and the UK have 29 votes. Smaller countries, like Cyprus and Slovakia, have four.

The European Commission Based in Brussels, the European Commission is rather like the civil service of the European Union, taking care of the day-to-day running of the organisation. Almost 30,000 people work for the Commission, making it one of Europe's largest institutions. The Commission does several different jobs. It:

- **drafts proposals for new EU laws or policies,**
- **checks that EU laws and treaties are properly applied,**
- **begins legal action against member states or businesses that it believes are not following EU law.**

EU Commissioners Each member state appoints one or two commissioners to take responsibility for running one particular aspect of EU business.

There are 24 Commissioners in all. The current president, José Manuel Barroso is from Portugal, and former Labour MP, Peter Mandelson, is the UK representative. Currently he is EU commissioner for trade.

The European Parliament

There are 732 Members of The European Parliament (MEPs). In the course of a month, MEPs usually meet for one week in Strasbourg, and for two weeks, on committee work, in Brussels. Parliamentary support staff are based in Brussels and Luxembourg.

Powers Today, MEPs:
- **decide, with the Council of Ministers, on EU law,**
- **control more than half the money that the EU spends,**
- **watch over the European Commission and approve the appointment of all Commissioners.**

Elections The UK is allocated 78 of the 732 seats in the European Parliament. Of these Northern Ireland is allocated three seats. At the election in 2004, the Conservatives were the largest UK party in the European Parliament.

Voting In the UK, as in any other EU member state, voting in European Parliamentary elections is open to any EU citizen, provided they are on the local register of electors.

Contact Debates in the European Parliament are open to the public, and groups and individuals can visit the Parliamentary building. MEPs may be reached by e-mail or by post or phone at their constituency office.

Petitions All EU citizens have the right to submit a petition to the President of the European Parliament (the address is L-2929 Luxembourg) giving their view on a matter that is within the remit of the EU. The petition can be in any form – as long as it contains the sender's name, address, occupation, and signature.

■ BRIEF CASE

In 1999, the European Parliament ordered an investigation into fraud and corruption by members of the European Commission. The report of the investigation was very critical of the Commission and led to all 20 Commissioners resigning.

■ BRIEF CASE

Following a recent successful petition to the EU, the Greek authorities are now required to admit EU citizens to their museums under the same conditions as Greek nationals.

Today in the UK, MPs and judges still create and shape the law in much the same way as they have done for several hundred years. See law pages 114-115.

However our membership of the European Union requires all our laws to follow the treaties and agreements that we have made as members of the EU.

In this sense European law has become the most important source of law in the UK. This is not to say that all our law comes from Europe, but it does mean that all our current and future laws must not break the principles set out in the treaties that we have signed.

■ BRIEF CASE: Patricia

In 1994, British courts heard the case of Patricia Day who was made redundant after working for nearly five years as a part-time cleaner. Her employer, Hertfordshire County Council, stated that under UK law she was not entitled to any redundancy pay because she worked for less than 16 hours a week.

The judges decided that, although this practice did not break UK law it was a form of discrimination against women, as most of the part-time workforce was female.

As sex discrimination in employment was expressly forbidden in European Union law, the UK government had to change the law. Shortly afterwards the law was altered to give full and part-time workers similar employment rights.

The European Union

Law created through our membership of the European Union normally reaches us in four ways – through treaties, regulations, directives, and court judgements.

Treaties

Treaties are agreements made between our government and other EU member states, which become incorporated into our law by Parliament. Treaties often contain broad agreements on which further action will be based. Sometimes, however, they include sections that can have a very specific effect on people's lives.

■ BRIEF CASE

The Treaty of Rome, signed in 1957, is the agreement upon which the European Economic Community was established. Article 119 of the Treaty states that men and women should receive equal pay for equal work.

Regulations Regulations are the laws that put treaties into practice. Regulations automatically have effect in the UK, and no new national law is required.

Directives

Directives, like regulations, are a means of putting an EU objective into practice, but member states are able to choose for themselves how this will be done.

■ BRIEF CASE

An important section of the Treaty of Rome says that people should be able to move freely for work between member states. The regulations that have followed the Treaty require member states to introduce new laws to ensure this works. As a result, all member states needed to have laws granting visiting EU workers the same rights to education and housing as the citizens of their own state.

■ BRIEF CASE

In 2001, the EU issued a directive requiring companies operating in the EU to inform employees about any decision affecting their jobs – especially if it might lead to redundancy. This directive was made following a number of unexpected redundancies in France, issued by several multi-national companies. The UK was given seven years in which to implement the directive.

Court judgements The European Court of Justice considers all matters of European Community law. Located in Luxembourg, it is the most senior court in Europe and overrules all national courts. Member states must follow its decisions.

■ BRIEF CASE: John

Until recently, UK winter fuel payments were paid to women from the age 60, but not to men until they reached 65. This was challenged in the UK courts by retired postman John Taylor, who claimed it was unlawful discrimination. The British High Court asked the European Court of Justice to deliver a judgement on this in the light of European Community law. The European Court announced that this practice did not follow community law and that winter fuel payments should be given to men and women under the same terms.

• **Before you write, phone or ask for information, think carefully about exactly what you need to know. Don't be overlong in your explanation, keep to the most important details.**

• **If you are telephoning, you will probably first speak to a receptionist who may not be able to answer your question. Explain that you'd like to talk to someone about…(name the subject), and you should be put through. If they can't help, they may be able to give you the name of someone who can.**

• **It sometimes helps to put a few key words down on paper to remind you of what you want to say. You may also need a pen and paper to make a note of what you are told.**

• **It's a good idea to ask who you are talking to so, if you write or phone again, you know the name of the person you first spoke to.**

The following names and details are arranged according to the chapters in the main part of the book and are just a few of the many organisations that can help with the whole range of law-related problems.

General

A very useful guide to government and public services in Northern Ireland can be found at **www.onlineni.gov.uk**

Childline Northern Ireland, Memorial Building, 9-13 Waring Street, Belfast BT1 2EU. A free 24hr helpline for any child in danger or distress, tel 0800 1111. **www.childline.org.uk**

Children's Law Centre, Philip House, 123-37 York Street, Belfast BT15 1AB. Offers advice on children's rights and law relating to children and young people. The free advice line is open Mon-Fri 9am-5pm, tel 0808 808 5678. **www.childrenslawcentre.org**

Citizens Advice Bureau Northern Ireland, or CAB, gives free, confidential and independent information and advice on all kinds of problems. You can enquire by phone or at one of their offices in most towns and cities. For your nearest CAB, see the local phone book, **www.citizensadvice.co.uk** and for advice **www.adviceguide.org.uk**

Equality Commission for Northern Ireland, Equality House, 7-9 Shaftesbury Square, Belfast BT2 7DP, tel 028 9050 0600. Provides advice and assistance to people who believe they have been discriminated against on the grounds of their colour, race, nationality, ethnic or national origin – including being an Irish Traveller – religious belief, political opinion, sex, married status or because they have a disability. **www.equalityni.org**

Law Centre (NI), 124 Donegal Street, Belfast BT1 2GY, is an organisation which only accepts referrals from other organisation like the **CAB**. Do not contact them directly, but you may find some useful information on their website about their work to promote social welfare rights. **www.lawcentreni.org**

Law Society of Northern Ireland, Law Society House, 98 Victoria Street, Belfast BT1 3JZ, tel 028 90 231614, provides information on finding and using a solicitor and how to make a complaint against a solicitor. **www.lawsoc-ni.org**

Northern Ireland Commissioner for Children and Young People, Millennium House, 17-25 Great Victoria Street, Belfast BT2 7BA, tel 028 9031 1616, has a role to promote the rights and best interests of young people. They may be able to help with individual complaints especially relating to government services. **www.niccy.org**

Northern Ireland Human Rights Commission, Temple Court, 39 North Street, Belfast BT1 1NA, tel 028 9024 3987, provides advice and assistance to individuals on issues involving law or practice and the protection of human rights. **www.nihrc.org**

The Ombudsman. If you have a problem with your local authority, a government department, the health service, an insurance company, a bank or building society or a legal service, and are not happy with how your complaint has been dealt with, you can refer your case to the relevant ombudsman. You must first, however, have done everything you can to sort things out yourself with the person or organisation concerned. Your local **CAB** can explain how to submit a complaint, or you can contact the appropriate office at one of the addresses below. If the ombudsman decides your complaint is reasonable, the department or organisation responsible will be asked to do something about it - which might mean that you get an apology or compensation. New procedures may also be put into place to make sure the same thing doesn't happen again.

The Northern Ireland Ombudsman, 33 Wellington Place, Belfast BT1 6HN, tel 0800 34 34 24, **www.ni-ombudsman.org.uk**, for government departments and public bodies including the Health Service and District Councils; the **Financial Ombudsman Service**, South Quay Plaza, 183 Marsh Wall, London E14 9SR **www.obo.org.uk**; the **Police Ombudsman**, New Cathedral Buildings, St Anne's Square, 11 Church Street, Belfast BT1 1PG, tel 084 5601 2931 or 028 9082 8600, **www.policeombudsman.org**

Solicitors give advice on legal problems, take action for you on your behalf and represent you in many courts or tribunals (they may engage a barrister to appear in higher courts).

There are solicitors' offices in every town and city in Northern Ireland. Many solicitors take publicly funded or conditional fee cases, and some will give you a free introductory interview. However when you first make contact, it's important to ask how much the work will cost. Choosing the right firm of solicitors is important. The Law Society, the Just Ask! website or your local CAB can give you the name of firms specialising in cases involving your particular problem.

Life	SEX, CONTRACEPTION, PREGNANCY AND ABORTION

AFLaGA (formerly Rank Outsiders), BCM Box 8431, London WC1N 3XX, can give advice and support to serving and ex-serving members of the armed forces who are lesbian or gay. The helpline, tel 0870 740 7755, operates Wed 7-9pm & Sun 9am-7pm, but messages can also be left outside this time. **www.aflaga.org.uk**
British Agencies for Adoption and Fostering, Saffron House, 6-10 Kirby Street, London EC1N 8TS, tel 020 7421 2600 offer advice and information on adoption and fostering and can put you in touch with an office near you. **www.baaf.org.uk**
You can find details of **Northern Ireland Fostering and Adoption Services** at **www.childrensservicesnorthernireland. com**, or in the phonebook under Adoption and Fostering.

British Pregnancy and Advisory Service, has over 40 centres in Great Britain (none in Northern Ireland) able to provide pregnancy tests, consultation and emergency contraception, and to undertake abortions. For BPA's Actionline tel 0845 7 30 40 30. **www.bpas.org**

Brook Advisory Centres, offer free and confidential advice and counselling on sex and contraception for young people under 25, covering the whole of the UK. The Belfast centre is at 29a North Street, Belfast, BT1 1NA, tel 028 9032 8866. An advice line is open Mon- Fri 9am-5 pm, tel 0800 0185 023. **www.brook.org.uk**; 24 hour recorded info, tel 020 7950 7700.

Carafriend Helpline, PO Box 44, Belfast, tel 028 9032 2023. Offers advice and assistance to lesbians and gay men. Gay Helpline, tel 028 9032 2023, Mon-Wed 7.30pm-10pm. Lesbian Line, tel 028 9023 8668, Thurs 7.30pm-10pm. **www.cara-friend.org.uk**

Central Services Agency, 2 Franklin Street, Belfast BT2 8DQ, tel 028 9032 4431 provides information about local GPs, dentists, opticians, chemists and medical cards. **www.centralservicesagency.com**

Contact Youth, 139 Ravenhill Road, Belfast BT6 8DR, tel 028 9045 7848. Offers counselling and advice on all issues for young people, aged 11-25, and is run by staff members and trained volunteers. Youthline is a free confidential helpline, tel 0808 808 8000 open Mon-Fri 4pm-9pm.

fpaNI (formerly Family Planning Association NI), 113 University Street, Belfast BT7 1HP, tel 028 90 325 488 and 3rd Floor, 67 Carlisle Road, Derry, BT48 6JL, tel 028 71 260 016. Offers help or information about issues concerning sexual health, contraception, family planning services or planning or preventing a pregnancy. The Helplines are open Mon-Thurs 9am-5pm, Fri 9am-4.30pm. **www.fpa.org.uk**

Gay & Lesbian Youth Northern Ireland (GLYNI), tel 028 9027 8636. Offers support to young lesbians, gay men and bisexuals aged 16-25. **www.glyni.org.uk**

Southern Health and Social Services Board (SHSSB). Information and advice on sexual health including a directory of services available in Northern Ireland. **www.coolsexinfo.org.uk**

HIV and AIDS

HIV Support Centre, 7 James Street South, Belfast BT2 8ND. Provides information and support for people with HIV and AIDS in Northern Ireland, tel 0800 137 437 Mon-Fri 9am-5pm and 7pm-10pm, Sat 2pm-5pm. **www.thehivsupportcentre.org.uk**

The Rainbow Project, Floor 2, 2-6 Union Street, Belfast BT1 2JF and 37 Clarendon Street, Derry/Londonderry BT48 7ER, tel 028 9031 9030. Provides support for gays, lesbians and bi-sexuals and to those with AIDS/HIV. **www.rainbow-project.org**

DRUGS AND ADDICTION

FRANK (formerly the National Drugs Helpline), a 24hr free confidential helpline providing advice and information on all types of drug taking for drug users, their family and friends as well as information on local agencies, tel 0800 77 66 00, email: frank@talktofrank.com. **www.talktofrank.com**

Health Promotion Agency for Northern Ireland, 18 Ormeau Avenue, Belfast BT2 8HS, tel 028 9031 1611 has information on drugs and alcohol including a directory of useful contacts. **www.drugsalcohol.info**

Insight is a drug and alcohol information and resource unit. It provides information and advice for concerned friends or family or users, and those seeking help themselves. It is an outreach of Carlisle House, drug and alcohol rehabilitation unit, tel 028 9023 1173.

Narcotics Anonymous, tel 020 7730 0009, a confidential helpline, open 10am-10pm, seven days a week, for those trying to recover from addiction. **www.ukna.org**

Release, 388 Old Street, London EC1V 9LT; information and legal advice service on drug-related problems, Mon-Fri, 10am-6pm, tel 020 7729 5255, email: info@ release.org.uk. Provides legal advice and heroin helpline. Overnight & weekend helpline, tel 0845 4500 215. **www.release.org.uk**

HEALTH

Health and Social Services Councils give advice to anyone who feels they have a complaint about any aspect of the health services. Under 'H' in the phone book.

use the law with care try talking first

Northern Ireland Association for Mental Health, 80 University Street, Belfast BT7 1HE, tel 028 9032 8474. Is a voluntary organisation providing services for those with mental health needs, their carers, mental health professionals and other agencies, both statutory and voluntary. These include housing services, home support, advocacy services, counselling, information services, public education and research. **www.niamh.co.uk**

Samaritans, will talk to anyone needing emotional support or feeling suicidal. You can say what you like, you need not give your name, it's entirely confidential. They can be reached by phone at any time, every day of the year. The central number is 08457 90 90 90 or, for your local branch, look under 'S' in the phone book. **www.samaritans.org.uk**

Sane, 1st Floor, Cityside House, 40 Adler Street, London E1 1EE, tel 020 7375 1002, able to provide information and advice to anyone (including friends and family) suffering mental health problems. They can also give callers the names of solicitors prepared to give up to an hour's free advice and put them in touch with support available in their local area. A helpline operates every day of the year between 12noon-2am, tel 0845 767 8000. **www.sane.org.uk**

Safety

PERSONAL SAFETY

Belfast Rape and Sexual Abuse Crisis Centre, 29 Donegall Street, Belfast, tel 028 9032 9901; helpline 028 9032 9002.

Kidscape, 2 Grosvenor Gardens, London SW1W 0DH, tel 020 7730 3300, provides free information and advice on keeping safe, including bullying and how to cope with it, open Mon-Fri 10am-4pm. **www.kidscape.org.uk**

Survivors UK, 2 Leather Market Street, London SE1 3HN, tel 0845 122 1201, email: info@survivorsuk.org.uk. A helpline is open Mon-Tues 7-10pm, giving advice and information to men who are victims of sexual violence. **www.survivorsuk.org**

Suzy Lamplugh Trust, Hampton House, 20 Albert Embankment, London SE1 7TJ, tel 020 7091 0014, email: trust@suzylamplugh.org. Practical information, guidance and resources on personal safety in all situations. **www.suzylamplugh.org**

VICTIMS AND COMPENSATION

The Compensation Agency, Royston House, 34 Upper Queen Street, Belfast BT1 6FD, tel 028 9024 9944. Provides compensation for victims of crimes of violence in Northern Ireland. Write or phone for information and application forms. **www.compensationni.gov.uk**

The Northern Ireland Court Service, The Information Centre, Windsor House, 10-12 Bedford Street, Belfast BT2 7LT, tel 028 9032 8594. Provides information about using the courts in Northern Ireland, open Mon-Fri 9.30am-4.30pm. **www.courtsni.gov.uk**

Victim Support, Annsgate House, 70/74 Ann Street, Belfast BT1 4EH, tel 028 9024 4039. There is a helpline providing support to people who have been victims of crime, Mon-Fri 9am-9pm and Sat-Sun 9am-7pm, tel 0845 30 30 900. **www.victimsupport.com**

Education

Department of Education, Rathgael House, 43 Balloo Road, Bangor, Co Down BT19 7PR, tel 028 9127 9279. Provides information on educational provision in Northern Ireland. **www.deni.gov.uk**

Education Otherwise, PO Box 325, Kings Lynn, PE3Y 3XW, provides information and advice for people choosing to educate their children out of school, tel 0870 730 0074, email: enquiries@education-otherwise.org **www.education-otherwise.org**

The five **Education and Library Boards** are responsible for local administration of schools, youth services and libraries. They can be found in the phonebook under "E" for Education.

SKILL in Northern Ireland, Unit 2 Jennymount Court, North Derby Street, Belfast BT15 3HN, tel 028 9028 7000. Gives information and advice to disabled students or those with learning difficulties about all aspects of education and training for people aged 16 and over. **www.skill.org.uk**

Work and Training

Department for Employment and Learning, Adelaide House, 39/49 Adelaide Street, Belfast BT2 8FD, tel 028 9025 7777. Provides information on training and employment law. **www.delni.gov.uk/er**

Employers for Childcare, 87 Main Street, Moira BT67 0LH, run an advice line for expectant and new parents, tel 028 9261 0661. Offering information and referral service on issues including parents legal rights, childcare and tax credits. **www.employersforchildcare.org**

Equality Commission for Northern Ireland – see general section.

Health and Safety Executive for Northern Ireland, Information and Advice Centre, 83 Ladas Drive, Belfast BT6 9FR, tel 028 9024 3249, is responsible for checking health and safety at work in Northern Ireland. Provides advice and information explaining the law and can tell you who to contact if you have a health and safety problem with training or at work. A free helpline is open Mon-Thurs 9am-5pm, Fri 9am-4.30pm, tel 0800 0320 121. **www.hseni.gov.uk**

Lesbian and Gay Employment Rights (LAGER), Unit 1g, Leroy House, 436 Essex Road, London N1 3QP, tel 020 7704 2205 advising lesbians and gay men encountering discrimination at work because of their sexuality, tel 020 7704 8066 (lesbian rights) and 020 7704 6066 (gay men). **www.lager.dircon.co.uk**

National Minimum Wage Helpline (Northern Ireland) is operated by staff in the **Northern Ireland Association of Citizens Advice Bureaux (NIACAB)**, 11 Upper Cresent, Belfast BT7 1NT. Provides help and advice to employees and employers in matters relating to minimum wages. Helpline open Mon-Fri 10am-4pm, tel 0845 6500 207.

Money

Association of British Insurers, Consumer Information Dept., 51 Gresham Street, London EC2V 7HQ, tel 020 7600 3333, for leaflets and further information on insurance. **www.abi.org.uk**

use the law with care **try talking first**

Benefits, administered by the Department for Work and Pensions. For information on benefits, contact your local Jobcentre Plus or Social Security office listed in the phone book. The Social Security Agency runs a free Benefit Enquiry Line, tel 0800 220 674. **www.dsdni.gov.uk** and **www.jobcentreonline.com**

Consumerline, tel 0845 600 6262, Mon-Fri 9am-5pm, is supported by the Trading Standards Service and the General Consumer Council for Northern Ireland. It provides advice and information about consumer law and deals with general enquiries and consumer complaints. **www.consumerline.org**

Debtline NI, 0800 027 4990 (free), for confidential help with debt problems and advice packs. **www.debtlineni.org**

Department of Enterprise, Trade and Investment, Northern Ireland Trading Standards Service, 176 Newtownbreda Road, Belfast BT8 6QS, tel 028 9025 3900 is a government watchdog, protecting consumers' interests. **www.detini.gov.uk**

General Consumer Council For Northern Ireland, Elizabeth House, 116 Holywood Road, Belfast, BT4 1NY, tel 028 9067 2488 was set up by the Government to promote and protect the interests of consumers. It provides information and help as well as dealing with individual complaints about passenger transport, coal, natural gas and electricity. Complaints line tel 0845 601 6022. **www.gccni.org.uk**

Inland Revenue, free information leaflets on taxation and general enquiries are available from Beaufort House, 31 Wellington Place, Belfast BT1 6BH, tel 028 9050 5000, or from any Inland Revenue enquiry centre. Details from **www.inlandrevenue.gov.uk**

Family

The website **www.childrensservices northernireland.com** is a useful guide to a variety of services in Northern Ireland including adoption and childcare provision.

Childline Northern Ireland, Memorial Building, 9-13 Waring Street, Belfast BT1 2EU. A free 24hr helpline for any child in danger or distress, tel 0800 1111. **www.childline.org.uk**

Gingerbread Northern Ireland, 169 University Street, Belfast BT7 1HR, tel 028 9023 1417. Works with and for one parent families providing a range of services including an advice and information service, giving information on welfare benefits, family law, child support on the advice line, tel 0808 808 8090. Open Mon-Fri 9am-5pm (closed 1pm-2pm for lunch). **www.gingerbreadni.org**

Kidscape, 2 Grosvenor Gardens, London SW1W 0DH, tel 020 7730 3300, provides free information and advice on keeping safe, including bullying and how to cope with it, open Mon-Fri 9am-4pm, helpline tel 0845 120 5204 **www.kidscape.org.uk**

Message Home Helpline, a confidential service allowing someone who has run away from home to leave a message for family and friends to let them know they are alive and well and can make referrals, tel (free) 0800 700740. **www.missingpersons.org**

National Missing Persons Helpline 0500 700 700 provides help, information and advice to families of missing people. NMPH HQ, 284 Upper Richmond Road West, London SW14 7ZU, tel 020 8392 4590. **www.missingpersons.org**

National Society for the Prevention of Cruelty to Children (NSPCC), Jennymount Court, North Derby Street, Shore Road, Belfast BT15 3NH, tel 028 9035 1135. The NSPCC runs a free 24hr child protection helpline for children and young people, parents and anyone concerned about young people at risk, tel 0808 800 5000. **www.nspcc.org.uk**

NORCAP, 112 Church Road, Wheatley, Oxfordshire OX33 1LU, tel 01865 875 000, provides advice and support for adopted people and their birth relatives who wish to get in touch. Open Mon- Fri 10am-4.30pm. **www.norcap.org.uk**

Northern Ireland Legal Services Commission, 2nd Floor, Waterfront Plaza, 8 Laganbank Road, Mays Meadow, Belfast BT1 3BN, tel 028 9040 8888 can put you in touch with a local solicitor who can advise and represent you in matters concerning parental and other family relationships. **www.nilsc.org.uk**

Northern Ireland Women's Aid, 129 University Street, Belfast BT7 1HP, tel 028 9024 9041 provides refuge and emotional support to women and their children experiencing domestic violence within the home. 24 hour helpline 0800 917 1414. **www.niwaf.org**

Parentline Plus, 520 Highgate Studios, 53-79 Highgate Road, Kentish Town, London NW5 1TL, free tel 0808 800 2222, works with adults, children and young people providing information and support to families. **www.parentlineplus.org.uk**

Parents Advice Centre, Floor 4, Franklin House, 12 Brunswick Street, Belfast BT2 7GE, tel 028 9031 0891, offers support, guidance and counselling to parents and young people with any family problem. A free helpline is open Mon-Fri 10am-4pm and Mon-Thurs 7pm-9pm, tel 0808 8010 722, email: parents@pachelp.org. **www.pachelp.org**

Registrar General for Northern Ireland, Oxford House, 49-55 Chichester Street, Belfast BT1 4HL, tel 028 9025 2000. Provides access to birth records and offers advice on tracing birth parents. **www.groni.gov.uk**

Home

Housing Rights Service, Middleton Buildings, Fourth Floor, 10-12 High Street, Belfast BT1 2BA, tel 028 9024 5640. Provides free, independent, specialist advice, advocacy and representation on issues associated with homelessness, renting accommodation and housing debt. The advice is available Mon, Tue and Thurs 9.30am-4pm, Wed and Fri 9.30am-1pm. If you have a housing problem outside the opening hours you can contact Shelterline 24 hours a day for free on 0808 800 4444. **www.housing-rights.org.uk**

Northern Ireland Housing Executive, The Housing Centre, 2 Adelaide Street, Belfast BT2 8PB, tel 028 9024 0588 offers advice and support for a range of issues relating to housing. The Homeless Advice Centre, 32-36 Great Victoria Street, Belfast BT2 7BA, tel 028 90 317000, open Mon-Fri 9.30am-5pm, Thurs 1pm-5pm. Contact details for local and after hours homeless advice services can be found under "Housing Executive" in the phone book. **www.nihe.gov.uk**

Simon Community Northern Ireland, 57 Fitzroy Avenue, Belfast BT7 1HT, tel 028 9023 2882 provides accommodation and support services to single homeless people throughout Northern Ireland. Contact details for local direct access hostels can be found in the phone book. **www.simoncommunity.org**

Leisure

Citizencard, PO Box 1221, Newcastle-under-Lyme ST5 OUS, tel 0870 240 1221. Provide photo-ID card and proof of age card for under 18s for £5 and charge £9 for over 18s. **www.citizencard.net**

District councils can provide help and information about issues including access to the countryside, environmental health. You can find contact details in the phonebook.

Information about the licensing and use of fireworks in Northern Ireland can be found at **www.saferfireworks.com**

Proof of Age Card Scheme, The Portman Group, 7-10 Chandos Street, Cavendish Square, London W1G 9DQ, tel 020 7907 3700. If you're 18 or over you can get a Proof of Age Card from the Portman Group for £5, tel 020 7907 3700. **www.portman-group.org.uk**

The Environment and Heritage Service is responsible for the environment, the built and natural heritage. There is a free 24hr emergency phone line on which you can report any environmental pollution incident, tel 0800 80 70 60. **www.ehsni.gov.uk**

The Northern Ireland Countryside Access and Activities Network (CAAN), The Stableyard, Barnett's Demesne, Belfast BT9 5PB, tel 028 90303930 is an umbrella organisation which brings together all groups and bodies with an interest, or involvement in countryside recreation in Northern Ireland. **www.countrysiderecreation.com**

Ulster Society for the Prevention of Cruelty to Animals (USPCA), PO Box 103, Belfast BT6 8US, tel 028 9081 4242 provides advice on animal welfare. You can contact them to report an animal in distress. **www.uspca.co.uk**

Travel and transport

ABTA (The Association of British Travel Agents), 68-71 Newman Street, London W1T 3AH, for information and advice over problems with a package holiday, tel 020 7637 2444, email: information@abta.org.uk. For general travel information, tel 0901 201 5050 (calls charged at 50p per minute). **www.abtanet.com**

DVLNI, County Hall, Castlerock Road, Coleraine BT51 3TA, for enquiries about driving licences, tax discs or the registration details of a particular vehicle. There is a 24 hour enquiry line, tel 028 9025 0500. **www.dvlni.gov.uk**

DVTA, 12 Balmoral Road, Belfast BT12 6QL, for information on driving motorcycle tests. Costumer helpline 0845 601 4094 open Mon–Fri 9am –5pm. **www.doeni.gov.uk/dvta**

Euro<26 Card, see National Youth Agency site at **www.nya.org.uk/euro26**

Royal Society for the Prevention of Accidents Northern Ireland (RoSPA NI), Nella House, Dargan Crescent, Belfast BT3 9JP, tel 028 9050 1160. Information on safety on the road and in the home. **www.rospa.com**

Translink, Central Station, Belfast BT1 3PB, tel 028 9066 6630. The main provider of public transport in Northern Ireland. Information on train and bus services and discount travel schemes. **www.translink.co.uk**

Young Persons Railcard, ATOC Ltd, 3rd Floor, 40 Bernard Street, London WC1N 1BY. **www.youngpersons-railcard.co.uk**

Citizens Advice Bureau (CAB), have trained staff who can give free legal advice and suggest solicitors able to deal with your particular problem. See **General** section, for contact details.

Police Ombudsman for Northern Ireland, New Cathedral Buildings, St. Anne's Square, 11 Church Street, Belfast BT1 1PG, tel 028 9082 8600 is the official body overseeing complaints against the police and can provide information on how to make a complaint if you have witnessed or suffered police misconduct.
www.policeombudsman.org

The Northern Ireland Court Service, Information Centre, Windsor House, 10-12 Bedford Street, Belfast BT2 7LT, tel 028 9032 8594. Provides information explaining how the court system works and what you can expect if you are charged with a criminal offence or attend court as a witness, a member of a jury or as a defendant or plaintiff in a civil case in Northern Ireland. Open Mon-Fri 9.30am-4.30pm. **www.courtsni.gov.uk**

The Northern Ireland Criminal Justice System online is at **www.cjsni.gov.uk**

The Northern Ireland Legal Services Commission, 2nd Floor, Waterfront Plaza, 8 Laganbank Road, Mays Meadow, Belfast BT1 3BN, tel 028 9040 8888 provides information on legal aid and maintain a directory of solicitors. **www.nilsc.org.uk**

The Northern Ireland Prison Service, Prison Service Headquarters tel 028 9052 2922; General Enquiry Point tel 028 9052 5265; Maghaberry Prison tel 028 9261 1888; Magilligan Prison tel 0290 7776 3311; Hydebank Wood tel 028 9025 3666. Email info@niprisonservice.gov.uk.
www.niprisonservice.gov.uk

The Probation Board for Northern Ireland, 80-90 North Street, Belfast BT1 1LD, tel 028 9026 2400. The operating service for probation in Northern Ireland providing pre-sentence reports to the courts, supervising offenders in the community and in prison and contributing to public protection through reducing offending.

Law, government and human rights

POLITICAL PARTIES

Alliance Party of Northern Ireland, 88 University Street, Belfast BT7 1HE, tel 028 9032 4274. **www.allianceparty.org**

Progressive Unionist Party, 299 Newtownards Road, Belfast, BT4 1AG, tel 028 9022 5040. **www.pup-ni.org.uk**

Sinn Féin, 51-55 Falls Road, Belfast, BT12 4PD, tel 028 9022 3000. **www.sinnfein.ie**

Social, Democratic and Labour Party, 121 Ormeau Road, Belfast BT7 1SH, tel 028 9024 7700. **www.sdlp.ie**

The Green Party, PO Box 281, Bangor, BT19 1NN, tel 0787 6597 900 **www.greens-in.org**

The Democratic Unionist Party, 91 Dundela Avenue, Belfast BT4 3BU, tel 028 9047 1155. **www.dup.org.uk**

Ulster Unionist Party, Cunningham House, 429 Holywood Road, Belfast BT4 2LN, tel 028 9076 5500. **www.uup.org**

United Kingdom Unionist Party, Parliament Buildings, Stormont, Belfast BT4 3XX, tel 028 9052 1482. **www.ukup.org**

GENERAL

House of Commons Information Office, House of Commons, London SW1A 0AA, tel 020 7219 3000. A public information service on the working and proceedings of Parliament. **www.parliament.uk**

Northern Ireland Assembly Public Information Office, Parliament Buildings, Belfast BT4 3XX, tel 028 9052 1333. **www.ni-assembly.gov.uk**

The Criminal Justice NI website provides links to the websites of the main statutory agencies in the system including the Police, the DPP, the Northern Ireland Office the Probation Board and the Northern Ireland Court Service. **www.cjsni.gov.uk**

The Electoral Office NI, St Anne's House, 15 Church Street, Belfast BT1 1ER, tel 028 9044 6688, provides information on how to register to vote and to apply for an Electoral Identity Card. **www.electoralofficeni.gov.uk**

The European Union

The Council of Europe, an organisation with a strong interest in human rights, which works to find solutions to some of the problems facing European society, Avenue de L'Europe, 67075 Strasbourg Cedex, France, tel +33(0)3 88 41 20 33, email: infopoint@coe.int; **www.coe.int**

European Commission, can indicate your nearest centre for information, tel 020 7973 1992. Representation in the UK, 8 Storey's Gate, London, SW1P 3AT, fax 020 7973 1900. **www.cec.org.uk**

The European Commission Office in Northern Ireland, 9-15 Bedford Street, Belfast BT2 7EG, tel 028 9024 0708, is a provider of information about the European Union. The EC Info-Point is open Mon-Thur 9.30am-5pm and Fri 9.30am-4.30pm. The Reference Library is open every afternoon from 2.30pm. **www.cec.org.uk/ni**

European Parliament Information Office, 2 Queen Anne's Gate, London SW1H 9AA, tel 020 7227 4300, email: eplondon@europarl.europa.eu For a free information service on the European Parliament, tel 00 800 678 91011. **www.europarl.org.uk**

European Youth Forum (EYF), represents youth organisations from all over Europe. **www.youthforum.org.**

Organising Bureau of School Students Unions (OBESSU), tel +32(0) 264 72 390, email: obessu@obessu.org, coordinates national organisations of schools and provides European representation for school students. **www.obessu.org.**

use the law with care try talking first